Praise for The 50 Things:

'Ever read something and thought, "Man, I wish I had written that?" Well once you get over that feeling, you are going to thank your lucky stars that this book is there to guide you in the most important conversations any parent can have with their kids. Supremely wise, funny, and totally practical . . . this may just be my new favourite book!!!'   Hugh Jackman

'This book is that rare thing: a non-preachy and super-helpful guide. Every page made me smile and some laugh aloud.'
                    Eoin Colfer, bestselling author of *Artemis Fowl*

'Humane, funny and above all loving. I wish I'd written it to my children.'   Fiona Bruce

'Few exude the love warmth, humour, humility, and insight-fulness we all aspire to, as naturally and generously as Peter Dunne and I can't recommend the soul-warming experience of reading his wonderful blog-born, hence uncontrived, book highly enough.'   Stephen Russell, aka The Barefoot Doctor

'This is a book for the ages. As you read it, you think, why didn't somebody do this a long time ago? Every father should have it and every child should read it.'   Jim Sheridan

'A book to be kept in your back pocket at all times!'
                                                    ~ 'ope Wilton

THE 50 THINGS

THE 50 THINGS

THINGS

Lessons For When
You Feel Lost, Love Dad

PETER DUNNE

TRAPEZE

An Orion paperback

First published in Great Britain in 2017
by Trapeze
This paperback edition published in 2018
By Trapeze, an imprint of The Orion Group Ltd,
Carmelite House, 50 Victoria Embankment,
London EC4Y ODZ

An Hachette UK company

1 3 5 7 9 10 8 6 4 2

A CIP catalogue record for this book is available
from the British Library.

ISBN (Paperback): 978 1 409 16791 4

Typeset by carrdesignstudio.com

Printed in Great Britain by Clays Ltd St Ives plc

The Orion Publishing Group's policy is to use papers
that are natural, renewable and recyclable products and
made from wood grown in sustainable forests. The logging
and manufacturing processes are expected to conform to
the environmental regulations of the country of origin.

www.orionbooks.co.uk

This book is dedicated to my heartbeats
Charlie, Amelia and Esme.
With all my love.

ॐ परमा मने नमः

THE 50 WHAT?

In July 2013, just like a lot of people born in 1963, I turned fifty years old. Of course that is a commonplace occurrence that falls to many people every single day, so while it was unique to me, and kind of fun to have a birthday with an 'o' in it, it wasn't something to which I had given much thought. In fact, as far as I was concerned, I was happy and ready to leave my forties behind me. I felt I was in good shape, physically, and while my career success always seems to teeter on a razor's edge, I was holding up. As the saying goes, things could have been worse. But deep down something was niggling, and I couldn't work out what it was.

How this discontent manifested is, in itself, somewhat curious. Would we call it a mid-life crisis? Not really. I mean, I didn't go out and buy a new car, or get an alarming new haircut or a new wardrobe. Nor did I have torrid affairs with women half my age. (At this point, everyone who knows me is shaking their head and saying, 'As if.')

What happened was this: I started to measure things. I began to think about the fact that I had clocked up a half-century. What had I accomplished? At first sight it was a list that seemed more noteworthy for what I had not managed to do, rather than anything else. For example, I had patently failed to invent the internet; I had not been orbited into outer space; nor had I found the solutions to climate change, the Middle East problem, Third World hunger or a cure for cancer. And having found none of those things, nor had I been as successful as Richard Branson or Steve Jobs or any of the other billionaire entrepreneurs who, like me, had skipped tertiary education.

As that rather disappointing conversation chuntered on in my head, I then had that glorious moment of revelation which, I imagine, was a bit like a big slap between the eyes with a wet fish.

And it was this. That my life's most amazing achievement is that I am the father of three incredible people: Charlie, now nineteen, Amelia, sixteen, and Esme, fourteen – my beautiful children, all of them smarter, kinder and more warm-hearted than me. And, most gratifying of all, they tolerate my attempts at humour with great understanding and compassion.

So that was it. I could have stopped the conversation with myself right there, but then a really funny thing happened. I had a conversation with my friend Steve.

Steve is one of my best friends. We worked together in the international division of a film studio in London in the early 2000s, and our friendship was forged in the searing white heat of a global marketing campaign. Our boss had retired two months ahead of the launch and we were thus somewhat abandoned. Our nearest boss was 6000 miles away at head office and the eight-hour time difference, and the time-sensitive pressures of the job at hand, meant that we were both making decisions far above our respective pay grades as we got closer to the kick-off. In that intense pressure we had to trust one another completely, and as a result, having come through it without either of us failing the other, we were destined to be friends for life.

So fast-forward again, to the time of my fiftieth birthday: Steve had just come through a lengthy divorce process and, as we recollected my fortieth birthday party – a huge, proper party with a glitter-ball disco and everything – I started to open up about being fifty and trying to work out what I had achieved.

And dear Steve, who can read me like a book and could tell I was struggling, said, 'You have just turned fifty. You need to write something great and lasting for your kids. Write down the fifty things you want them to remember when you are gone, like a handbook for life.'

That was when the penny dropped, and I suddenly knew that that was exactly what I was going to write. You see, when you get to fifty, you're not playing any more. By any margin, you're probably past the halfway point to wherever it is you're heading and, at the end of it all, what do we leave behind? How do we know we're leaving the world a better place? I knew I was leaving my best work – my children – but supposing I forgot to tell them something really important?

But there is another reason that the idea resonated so well with me. I think it's to do with the fact I was raised by parents who, while loving, were dealing with issues of their own and were maybe not as steady as I sometimes needed them to be. I grew up trying to work out my own reference points, my own map of the universe, and while it has done the job, I knew that I wanted to leave my children with a better map; or a guide to their own maps, so that they could get where they want to go that bit faster, perhaps without so many painful lessons.

So it's all down to Steve, really, so thank you, chum, and welcome to *The 50 Things*.

Peter Dunne

AN OPEN LETTER
TO MY CHILDREN

Hi guys,

I'm writing this in the study at home. I can hear Amelia playing table tennis outside and, a bit further away, Charlie is playing footie with some friends. Mum and Esme are on their way home from Devon and it's a quiet, happy-go-lucky kind of day. The dogs are sprawled around me in a big heap, and in a while I'll walk them around the fields and think about what we might have for dinner tonight.

It's a couple of years since I turned fifty, and a couple of months since I finished writing the last instalment of *The 50 Things*. It has been a fairly challenging process, and some of the things I thought would be hard to write about were the easiest, while others baffled me for a few weeks before I found my voice. But every chapter came about through the same process: intuition.

Sure, I made a list of fifty topics I wanted to write about, but I had no plan for the order in which I would write them, nor what I would say. Having identified the next topic I reflected on it, mainly while driving, and filed the ideas away in the back of my mind, waiting for the moment when I simply could not avoid writing for another minute. Once the gestation process was over, I would find a way to hook myself into the topic – sometimes a definition, sometimes a quotation – and then I would launch myself into mid-air and hope for a soft landing. And once I had written the first one, I had to work out what to do with it. Was it just for you guys? If so, why not just email it? But I realised that in writing this I was declaring my hand, not just about my love for you as your father, but on every single one of the issues I wrote about, so I decided to start a blog. I have to admit I was nervous, but the responses from people who read the blog were unanimously warm and positive. Everyone seemed to recognise something in what I was trying to say, regardless of whether they were yet a parent themselves.

Because, you know how I said that turning fifty didn't really mean that much to me? Well, turns out it did. It struck me very hard that I am more than likely over halfway through my life – not that I want to be morbid – and I've been thinking about the things I have and haven't done and the things I might still do. And I worked out that if I can do anything of real value in this life, it might be to leave a trail of breadcrumbs for all of you to follow, so that if stuff comes up – and trust me, it's going to – you will have a note from me, a chance to refer back to what I thought on things that are important to me, and hopefully to you.

It's not compulsory. You don't even need to read it now. I just wanted to leave you – just in case I'm not always around to talk to – some user-friendly guidance, a kind of handbook for life, to help you cut through the jigs and the reels of the daily grind and get to where you want that little bit faster. You see, the thing that continues to drive me crazy about my own life is that, after all these years, I'm still trying to work it out. I feel as though I'm still crazy-paving my way down a yellow-brick road in pitch-darkness, while all around me others are doing the same, but making it look so much more accomplished. Sometimes I feel as though I'm still waiting to begin, for things to get started the way I want them to, and all the while the clock is ticking relentlessly on. And at some point soon someone is going to declare that I'm just too old to be bothered with any more.

But there was another thing that inspired me, and it was this: I reminded myself that when you were all tiny, our bedtime routine invariably included a bottle of warm milk and a story, snuggled up in bed, safe and protected from the world. And sometimes, in addition to the story, we would review the day and recall all the things that had happened. As the song says, we'd minimise the negative, accentuate the positive, reinforce good life lessons and try to set you up for a night of sweet dreams. One night as I finished the story, I got up to go and Charlie, who would have been about four, said, 'Daddy, can you do the Day-It-Is?'

At first I thought you said, 'Daddy, can you do the Deities?' and I was wondering what the hell I was going to come up with for that! But, of course, the name stuck, though time moved on and you all grew up. So, in a way, this is your own grown-up version of the 'Day-It-Is', only now it's called *The 50 Things*.

Whatever the subject, I promise you one thing: I don't know anything. Furthermore, anyone who tells you he knows anything is either deluded or dishonest, and best avoided.

The truth is, as someone really smart (Socrates or Plato, I think) once said, 'The man who claims he knows, knows nothing; the man who claims nothing, knows.'

Just think about it.

I love you.

Dad x

THE 1ST OF 50 THINGS

COMPROMISE

'Compromise, if not the spice of life, is its solidity.
It is what makes nations great and marriages happy.'
Phyllis McGinley

COMPROMISE

When I was imagining my first entry, I thought it would be about something big like sex, religion or politics, but I had a sudden impulse to write about Compromise instead and maybe it's not such a bad idea. If your lives are going to be like anyone else's, the sooner you get friendly with Compromise, the better. I've had a long career in the film industry, working alongside some of the richest, most successful and most famous people on the planet, and I can't think of one of them who gets their own way all the time. I have many amusing (and some not so amusing) anecdotes about people who struggled with that concept, and they've convinced me that it's never a good thing to feel absolutely entitled to getting one's own way. And as in show business, so it is in politics: as president of the USA, Barack Obama was the most powerful person on the planet, but his domestic agenda was continuously disrupted by the Republican majority in the Senate, which caused him no end of grief. Even he didn't get to have it all his own way. And somehow there is something very sad and unhealthy about someone who gets too much of their own way. It creates a kind of neurosis that bursts out when life throws them a curve ball. I want you to be able to get through life without having a breakdown if you don't get your own way. That's why I think Compromise is important.

Compromise is an old person's word. When I say 'old' I am talking about anyone over the age of thirty. By thirty you have hopefully grasped that you are possibly not operating from the geographical centre of the universe, that life does not always go your way and that you just may, sometimes (often, actually) have to adjust your aims and your expectations and learn to deal with the disappointment that it brings. Before thirty, you may think you are the master of the universe and you spend a lot of time being aghast that God/the universe/everyone you know has not recognised this fact and brought you all you demand on silver platters while carrying you around on a bejewelled bier. Or was this just me?

But, if you are lucky, by the time you get to thirty this permanent and unpleasant state of surprise begins to pale and you start to get over yourself. (On the other hand, if, by thirty, you have not embraced Compromise then you are probably a megalomaniac or sociopath and doing very well in the entertainment business, judging from some of the people I've met!)

Compromise is defined as 'a settlement of differences by mutual concessions, an agreement reached by adjustment of conflicting or opposing claims, principles, etc., by reciprocal modification of demands'.

So Compromise means that no one gets exactly what they want. We see it all the time in everyday life. The 2010–2015 UK Parliament was led by a coalition government between two political parties who had previously been in opposition. Just getting both sides of the coalition to agree to Compromise on a daily basis made the job of pushing government policies through Parliament a much more arduous process. Arguments raged over many topics, including environmental policy, the top rate of tax and university tuition fees. But, you know, I really believe that some of those policies were the better for being even more thoroughly debated and pulled apart. In fact, that's exactly what the democratic parliamentary process is based upon.

Similarly, in your real life, your personal relationships, Compromise is vital. One person cannot prevail at all times. For a start, it's unhealthy, and also, the relationship can't last very long under those conditions. Something, or more likely someone, is going to break down. In most instances you have to find a way for both of you to win. And sometimes you win by being happy that the other person is getting it their way.

As I've said, in my opinion getting your own way all the time is bad for you. It creates false expectation and discourages effort, be it in relationships or business or life generally.

Of course, there are certain things on which you can't Compromise. When King Solomon was presented with two mothers claiming the same newborn baby, his proposed Compromise was a fantastic bluff, but cutting babies in half is never going to be seen as a great success.

Likewise, you can't Compromise on things like your kid's name. You both have to love the name. You can't fake it. There was, I admit, a point when I thought Charlie would be better called Humphrey. But your mother didn't like it and that was that. And that was not a problem because we both had to love it or it was a non-starter.

But if you are in a loving relationship based on trust and respect, then you are safe to make big shifts towards one another. Sure, one person might be more persuasive – you've all seen your mother wrap me around her little finger – but you can't persuade someone to love something that they hate. The only way forward is to, say it with me: Compromise!

I heard a great joke about Compromise:

A guy tells his friend, 'My girlfriend wants a cat, but I don't like them, so we're going to compromise.'

'Oh really?' says his friend. 'How are you going to do that?'

'We're getting a kitten.'

And that, kids, may just be the most eloquent demonstration of Compromise ever.

KINDNESS

'Three things in human life are important: the first is to be kind;
the second is to be kind; and the third is to be kind.'

Henry James

KINDNESS

They say that in life you only regret the things you didn't do, rather than the things you did. (I could dispute that: there are plenty of things I regret doing, but maybe time will iron those out for me. For example, I really regret those sambucas on that last night in Greece.)

I mention that because I happened to read a brilliant address at Syracuse University in New York by a guy called George Saunders (google it!), in which he said that his only regrets were his failures of Kindness. And I really know what he means.

Kindness is a dark horse. It's a bit like your really dull cousin who goes into his bedroom a computer nerd and comes out five years later a rock star. What do I mean by that? Well, I mean that Kindness can often be ignored or overlooked because it's a bit old-fashioned and not very cool, and it's rarely impressive because it's based in tiny, little things: gestures, understandings and sometimes actions, rather than big, grandiose things. Yet for all its innate modesty, I would argue that it is the most important virtue there is.

Last winter, on a bitterly cold night in London I walked past a woman who was sitting on the pavement. Her dirty hand was half-cupped in that way homeless people half-cup their hands when hoping someone will give them money, but the thing that was most notable about her was that she was sobbing. Noticeably sobbing. Gut-wrenching sorrow was pouring out of her to the extent that I actually noticed. And wanted to help. I felt strongly compelled to kneel down and ask her if I could help, to offer her the very compassion and Kindness which, in her place, I know I would have wanted so badly.

But something stopped me.

I don't know if it was fear of embarrassment, fear of other people walking past on the street seeing me, or fear that I might catch her homelessness, her helplessness. I don't know. But, I'm ashamed to say, I wasn't the Good Samaritan; I was the guy who passed by on the other side. I'm not proud of it. I tell you of my failure only to make you aware that this can happen.

There's not an excuse I can think of not to have helped that woman, to have sat down and asked her what was wrong. Nothing is more important than a person's welfare. Seriously. And contrary to what certain people choose to believe, homeless people are generally not eccentric lottery winners. Sure, some are addicts, but that in itself is a cause for compassion rather than dismissal. And I suspect, no, I actually know this because it's ringing true in my heart as I write it to you, that what hurts them as much as the grinding poverty in which they are drowning, is the way in which the rest of humanity ignores them.

We know a few people who would have risen to that challenge that night. Your Uncle Anthony would have bent down and given the shirt off his back if he had been there, and he would have opened his heart to her, too. Not many people, me included, are that brave, but my old boss's wife, Sarah Chissick would have scooped her up. Your Auntie Mandy would have rushed off for fish and chips. Your father? I dropped a fiver and kept going to an appointment so important that I can't even remember it now.

The point is that every so often the universe will offer you a cubic centimetre of choice, a small window of opportunity for you to make a difference. And in this life there are going to be precious few of those.

So pay attention and, when the moment comes, don't be embarrassed. Be kind.

GRIEF

'Give sorrow words; the grief that does not speak knits up the
o-er wrought heart and bids it break.'
William Shakespeare, *Macbeth*

GRIEF

This chapter was supposed to be about love but, as you know, life sometimes has other plans.

As I was preparing to write something eloquent about love, something beautiful that William Shakespeare or someone else hasn't already said, something happened that changed the world. It depends where you are standing as to whether this is a tsunami or a puddle splash, but for me, and I think for you, too, it was a tidal wave: Charlie's godfather, Guy, one of my oldest, best and dearest friends, passed away very suddenly and unexpectedly and, most awfully of all it seems, quite needlessly.

Like all momentous personal events in the twenty-first century, this most tragic loss was heralded by a text message.

I knew the moment I saw the message: 'Have you heard about Guy?' I made a phone call to learn that he had died as a result of not taking anticoagulants following a minor operation. It was mind-numbing, but I stalled my emotions in shock mode and kept it together for another twenty-four hours, until the moment that another mutual friend told me that Guy frequently talked about us, about our family. I think that was the trigger, because Guy lived such a hectic, peripatetic existence that we rarely saw one another, and it was easy to think his life might have moved away from us. But when I was reminded that the long periods apart did not mean we were not close, that out of sight did not mean out of mind, when I was reminded of that, reminded of what we meant to him and what he meant to us, to me, that was when I broke down and wept.

Guy was not like anyone else I've ever known. We first met when he worked for a Non-Governmental Organisation concerned with preserving the environment for endangered species; he was ex-special forces; later on he would work in areas that most of us never think about, let alone travel to. He was an expert marksman who loved Barry Manilow music; he made Charlie's first teddy bear; he was never without a beautiful girlfriend; he could talk about astronomy and philosophy as well as his favourite Harry Potter book. All of this he did with 100 per cent of his being. Nothing he did was ever half-hearted. And this energy, this enthusiasm, was infectious to all who met him. Watching him was like watching a comet blaze past on its way to another galaxy. But blaze past it did, and, as suddenly as it came, so he left us.

Grief is a train wreck of an emotion. It trumps everything. And it gives you perspective like nothing else ever can.

Weirdly, Grief is perfectly capable of running alongside all your other emotions.

When your Grandma Jeannie was dying of cancer, your mum was pregnant with Charlie and we were waiting to move into our new house. It was perfectly possible then to be really happy and really sad at the same time. Exhausting, but possible.

And that's how it has been this week. I've been thinking so much about Guy and laughing about the things we did together. Our first meeting was a huge comedy of errors. Guy was coming with his charity colleagues to talk about a partnership with the film company I worked for, only I had completely forgotten they were coming and hadn't booked a conference room, and as they were doing their presentation, I managed to knock over a milk jug and a sugar bowl. Disasters like that make or break you, and we laughed like drains and became firm friends. Guy was fond of quoting his dad, Alan, who said that the best anecdotes are borne out of mishaps. That was never more true than the time we went walking in the Brecon Beacons and camped out in the forest only to be awoken by a rave at two o'clock in the morning! And all these stories line up waiting to be remembered, and suddenly I get a rabbit punch in the back of the head reminding me that he's gone, and that we will never see him again. The fact is so completely incomprehensible in that moment, and that sense of loss is so bereaving, so powerful, so devastating and so breathtaking, that there is nothing to do but let it consume you and flow with it.

And I think if there is any single thing I want you to take away from this, it's exactly that. You cannot fight this one. You have to go with it. And that's OK. In fact, it is exactly how it's meant to be.

From experience, I can tell you how it goes from here: for a while Grief takes over as your default operating software until, somehow, you begin to accommodate the loss of your loved one, and it moves backstage, always there but not as painful. I believe the Queen Mother once remarked, 'It never gets better, you just get better at it.'

Ultimately, there is an incipient beauty to Grief. Somehow, as it is expelled from your body, it purifies you. I don't mean to sound dramatic but truly, Grief changes you exactly as your love for the departed person changed you. 'Grief is,' as the Queen said at the memorial service for the victims of 9/11, 'the price we pay for love.'

Seen in that context, and given what I gained from my remarkable and wonderful friendship with Guy, I would still say it's a price I'm willing to pay.

LAUGHTER

'The best kind of laughter is when you start laughing for no reason and can't stop. In that moment, you forget about everything else. You let go of the world, and let go of control – which we all should do sometimes.'

Miley Cyrus

LAUGHTER

Laughter is a very important part of the daily diet. Never mind five fruit and veg a day. I mean, that's important, too, but this is real nourishment at a whole different level. It's the stuff that will feed your spirit and enhance the moments of your life that would otherwise be without meaning.

Seriously, think about how great it is to really laugh. Real Laughter comes from deep in your belly and rolls out of you in waves, carrying everyone with it. I'm talking about unconfined joy. And if you think about it, it's a natural state: every time you get together with your friends and those you love, Laughter is a natural occurrence that just bubbles up between people. Watch next time you are out and about: everywhere you look, people are laughing at nothing much. It's glorious!

This universe is pretty incredible, but sometimes that can get forgotten in the daily grind of getting through life.

That's where Laughter comes in. I believe Laughter raises your energy; it lifts you up and takes you to a place where more things are possible, where better choices are available. But even if I'm wrong and it does neither of those things, it leaves you feeling a great deal better than you did before you started.

Recently, I found an unmarked cassette tape and, when I managed to listen to it, it was an old recording of Charlie talking to your Uncle Tim. Charlie would have been about two years old when the recording was made, and Uncle Tim was reducing him to paroxysms of Laughter with his impersonation of a parrot. It made your mum and me laugh out loud when we played it, hearing Charlie gasping for breath as he said, 'Again, again,' in between gales of Laughter. It was truly joyous.

Likewise, that time Amelia got hold of the cream squirter and sprayed your cousin Ned a mouthful of whipped cream. In the photograph of that (rather messy) moment, the sheer delight of their Laughter is self-evident, Amelia's head thrown back like a hyena that's just heard the funniest joke in the jungle, and Ned barely containing his joy, or the whipped cream!

But there are many different kinds of Laughter, and I need to be clear with you that I am talking about real, sincere Laughter that comes from a place of joy: I'm not talking about cynical, mocking kind of Laughter which doesn't enrich anyone. Sure, it can be funny in small doses but it doesn't feed your soul if you only ever derive amusement from someone else's misfortune or discomfort. I call that the 'humour of cruelty' and, trust me, it's not cool.

But there's more to Laughter than just having a good time. Real Laughter, real joy, can be one of the most effective tools of political subversion there is.

It's hard to watch evil in action and see no one doing anything about it. So we have to stand up to it, and one way is to laugh.

At the BAFTA ceremony following the 9/11 attacks, Stephen Fry reminded the world that it was now more important than ever for people to continue to make movies, to celebrate art, to laugh freely, to shine their light brightly and let the world see it, for to do otherwise would be to bow to terrorism, to the forces of darkness which would like to make us afraid and stop us from freely expressing ourselves.

What could be more powerful than Laughter, bellowed out loud to overwhelm and decry the forces of darkness? For while there are those who would say that such Laughter might trigger an unwelcome response, I would say this: if you stop laughing, they have already won. So you must raise your head and laugh loudly. Comedy and Laughter are vital in fighting these absurdities insidiously masquerading as received wisdom. This is why satire is so valuable, for an idea that cannot stand up to the scrutiny of Laughter simply cannot stand. Laughter will dissolve all manner of wickedness but that can only happen if you assert your right to laugh freely.

But as I said, even if I am wrong, at least you will feel better.

Now, in case all of that was a little bit heavy, I want to finish this by relating an incident from many years ago, which still makes me laugh today. I was spending Christmas with my dad and his second wife, Nuala, whose large and extended family had joined us for dinner. As tradition dictates, we feasted on roast turkey and baked ham before the Christmas pudding was brought to the table, blue brandy flames dancing around it as it was placed on the table. As the pudding was served with cream and brandy butter, we pulled our Christmas crackers and then began the usual telling of bad jokes and marvelling at the crappy items masquerading as gifts. Beside me, Nuala's mother, Eilish, put on her paper hat and attacked her Christmas pudding, not realising that the gift contained in her cracker had fallen into her pudding where it had been covered by the cream and brandy butter. Eventually, however, by dint of her spoon, this mishap was revealed and Eilish held out her spoon to examine the small plastic object which had fallen into her bowl. Now, if you happened to own a plastic charm bracelet, this was the perfect gift: a small plastic charm in the shape of a farmyard cockerel. Eilish was perplexed.

'Jesus, Mary and Holy Saint Joseph!' she exclaimed. 'I had a cock in my mouth and I nearly ate it.'

There was a moment of stunned silence and the table then erupted into Laughter. Eilish was still perplexed and held out the spoon for everyone to see.

'My God tonight!' she continued. 'Look at the size of that cock! I could have choked to death on the size of it.'

And on she went in this vein until we were all literally crying with Laughter.

Finally, one of the dinner guests leant across the table and said, 'I tell you this: if she did have a cock in her mouth, it's the only one she ever nearly ate!'

At this point, ambulances were called and we were taken to hospital. OK, that last part is not true but the rest of it absolutely is, and if that did not demonstrate Laughter for you, then we should give up now.

THE 5TH OF 50 THINGS

ANGER

'The tigers of wrath are wiser than the horses of instruction.'
William Blake, *The Marriage of Heaven and Hell*

ANGER

For most of my adult life I've been lucky enough to have a fairly distant relationship with Anger. I think part of that is down to over twenty years of Transcendental Meditation (a practice which I honestly believe has saved my life, if not my mind), and part of it is due to a profound awareness of the havoc that can be wrought when Anger remains unchecked – and worse still, the utter futility of that havoc.

Seriously, when I was growing up, watching people around me acting irrationally in the grip of Anger was like witnessing insanity. How are you supposed to respect someone you've just seen screaming at an inanimate object? To paraphrase Anthony de Mello, it's about as productive as trying to teach a pig to sing. Firstly, it's totally pointless. Secondly, it's frustrating. And thirdly, it upsets the pig.

If emotions were drinks, compromise would be a cup of tea, kindness would be hot chocolate and Anger would be whisky.

I'm not being pejorative about whisky. Like Anger, it's amazingly powerful: just as a drop of whisky can fire you up in an instant, so Anger can ignite and explode instantaneously.

And similarly, just as a moderate amount won't harm you, so an excess can kill you.

And that's the nub of it, really: uncontrolled, Anger can rampage through your psyche like a two-year-old with a sugar rush, laying waste to logic and reason and smashing through courtesy and protocol like a runaway locomotive. Because of its power, we identify totally with it; it becomes us.

Yet, used judiciously and with detachment, Anger can be an incredibly powerful force for good.

In 'The Marriage of Heaven and Hell', my favourite English poet William Blake said, 'The tigers of wrath are wiser than the horses of instruction.'

Which means what? Only that sometimes (I stress the word 'sometimes'), it is necessary to play the part of an angry person. Used in the right way, Anger can focus attention exactly where it needs to be, exactly when it needs to be there. Anger can be a valuable red flag that saves time and energy, even lives. You'll perhaps remember me shouting at you at some point in your childhood to put down the sharp knife or get away from the naked flame?

So I guess my question about Anger, whenever it presents itself to me, is this: 'How is this going to serve me or the situation I'm in?' Ninety-nine per cent of the time the answer is, 'It's not going to serve me,' and I disengage. And luckily it is rare for me to find that I can't get past it. I can count on the fingers of one hand the number of times in my life that I have been incapacitated by rage.

My point is, if I can master it then so can you. And I recommend that you learn this early. For just as the side effect of too much whisky is a hangover, an excess of Anger is exhausting. Not only that, it tends to make people avoid us.

Aristotle, who was a wise old buzzard by anyone's measure, had this to say on the subject: 'Anybody can become angry – that is easy, but to be angry with the right person and to the right degree and at the right time and for the right purpose, and in the right way – that is not within everybody's power and is not easy.'

And that's the key here, I think: although it takes enormous self-control to master your own Anger, it is essential that you do so, for the alternative is that your Anger will master you, and without a restraining hand Anger is vicious and destructive and ugly and will leave you and those around you with the worst of whisky hangovers.

TOLERANCE

'Bigots will not be tolerated.'
Anon, graffiti

TOLERANCE

Tolerance, sometimes known as forbearance, is defined as 'the ability or willingness to tolerate the existence of opinions or behaviour which one dislikes or with which one disagrees'. Tolerance is a bit like riding a unicycle: it looks easy enough to the untrained eye but it's a bugger to master.

And that's it really. It seems simple enough but it can really stick in your throat. In fact, just typing that sentence has brought up a load of stuff about which I don't feel tolerant at all!

Years ago I saw some graffiti on the wall of a loo which perfectly illustrates the dichotomy of Tolerance: 'Bigots will not be tolerated.'

It still makes me laugh because, as ideologies go, it so patently doesn't work. It can't be OK that I can tolerate you only if your beliefs exactly mirror mine. That's the opposite of Tolerance.

So Tolerance has to apply to everything or it fundamentally fails. If you're going to do it you have to embrace it, you have to give it heart and soul. You can't hold back from anyone because that's . . . well that's just intolerant, isn't it?

Don't worry, greater minds than mine have wrestled with this. John F. Kennedy said, 'Tolerance implies no lack of commitment to one's own beliefs. Rather it condemns the oppression or persecution of others.' So Tolerance is a bedrock of democracy then. I might not like your beliefs and your ideology, but I will fight for your right to believe it. And I will stand up to those who would deny you that right.

Conversely and, let's face it, not terribly helpfully, Somerset Maugham said, 'Tolerance is another word for indifference.'

Now, much as I respect Somerset Maugham, I'm with JFK on this one. I may not love your culture, your way of life, your religious or political beliefs, but Tolerance says I must allow them. Put it this way, if I cannot tolerate your intolerance, then I am as intolerant as I think you are.

Do you remember when you were little how we always used to tell you to try to give other people the benefit of the doubt. What we were really talking about was Tolerance. It's common for children to stick together but we really tried to help you see how important it is not to write people off because they are different or stand out. As the joke goes, every class of school-children contains at least one difficult kid no one can stand, and if you can't work out who it is, it must be you! So, let's suppose it is you? Wouldn't you want that very Tolerance being denied you?

At this point, feeling a little like the Vicar of Dibley after Alice has explained her worries about I Can't Believe It's Not Butter (google it, it's genius!), I have to step away from the Tolerance dichotomy and urge you just to take a deep breath and go with it.

Because, here's the thing: a world in which there is no Tolerance is going to go to hell in a hand basket pretty damn quick. Let me demonstrate: we live in an age where a lot of people carrying out atrocities and terrorist attacks are doing so in the name of Islam. As a result, a lot of people, including Donald Trump, want to perpetuate the belief that therefore all

Muslims are *potential* terrorists. But that's not right. It's a wicked lie. And while we must allow Donald the right to believe what he wants, we must strive for Tolerance even as our fear threatens to overwhelm us. At the end of the day, we're all brothers under the skin and *those* Muslims, *those* Jews, *those* Christians, *those* Syrian refugees, we're all one family and we have to learn Tolerance for one another.

As I've said, if you look around you will find many smart people eloquently expounding great reasons why Tolerance is akin to indifference and apathy, and who knows, they may be right.

But my instinct here is to tolerate them and to give the last word to JFK, who was a truly great, and tolerant, man:

> World peace, like community peace, does not require
> that each man love his neighbour – it requires
> only that they live together with mutual tolerance,
> submitting their disputes to a just and peaceful
> settlement.

THE 7TH OF 50 THINGS

COURAGE

'And as long as you wanna be courageous,
Promise you we're gonna see some changes.'
George The Poet

COURAGE

Courage, like a valid passport, is something without which you should never leave the house. You just never know when you are going to need it.

In my view – though I'm happy to be corrected – there are two main types of Courage. There is the kind that is akin to bravery, where people overcome their fears and act courageously to overcome the prevailing circumstances. The other kind of Courage is more often associated with fortitude, with not running away.

Let's deal with the first type first.

Margaret Thatcher said many things, and lots of people have really strong opinions about a lot of what she said, and normally I would avoid quoting anyone quite so polarising simply because it can be unhelpful when you're trying to make a point. However, what she said about Courage was spot on. She said it was important because, 'You must never appease a bully.'

You're all still at school, so you probably remember our car chats about bullying? I had one chat with each of you, and it was generally in Year 2 or 3, and it went like this: 'It is vital, when dealing with a bully, that you never step down. Somehow you must find your Courage and, to paraphrase Shakespeare, "screw it to the sticking-place". If someone threatens to hit you, let them, but then hit them back as hard as you can, immediately.'

When I first delivered that advice to Charlie, aged seven, he countered, not unreasonably, 'But, Dad, if I do that won't he hit me again?'

To which, of course, the answer was, 'Maybe, but if you don't hit him he will know that he can hit you whenever he wants.'

I'm not a big advocate of using violence to combat violence, but this is one area when I think it's vital. Bullying is about the psychology of fear, and you have to use your Courage and stand firm, even if you get hit in the process. I know this may seem controversial to some parents, but from my own experience I know it's true. As a child who abhorred and feared violence, I thought the smart thing to do was to appease the bully. Sadly, all that does is give him (or her) licence to bully at will, while you live in fear. The only thing bullies respect is strength, mainly because it's the one thing they know they lack. If I had known that when I was ten I might have found the Courage to stand up to children who felt stronger by bullying me. No matter, I know it now.

Likewise, in life – you know, that place you all think so different from school – you may meet bullies. And if you go on to social media sites, as I know you do, you may encounter cyberbullies, people who will try to belittle and deride you to separate you from your friends. They tend to be a little more subtle than your classmates, but they walk among us and seek to dominate good, trusting people by exploiting their fear. You can't punch them back so you have to find other strategies for dealing with them, and Courage must always be forefront in your arsenal.

Here's the thing: whether it's the school playground or Facebook, it's the same stuff, and the only way to deal with it is to find your Courage and stand up to them. It's not easy, it can really hurt, but you have to do it because once they realise you are not going to kowtow they will move on. With cyber-bullying I know that's really tough, but I guess your yardstick has to be this: am I letting someone else determine my movements, my self-expression, or in any unwelcome way moderate my life or my actions? Be true to yourself and know that they cannot prevail. And if it happens to you, tell someone. Tell me. We'll find a way to deal with it. It may be painful, but don't let them win. I say this because I have not always managed to achieve it, and I can therefore tell you from personal experience, giving in makes it much worse. Stand strong and let the storm roll where it will, but never try to appease them.

That's an example of the first kind of Courage and it leads fairly neatly to the second kind, about which Napoleon Bonaparte said, 'Courage isn't having the strength to go on – it is going on when you don't have strength.' That captures it perfectly.

Sometimes, not running away is much harder than simply scarpering. There have been many times in my life that I have contemplated just doing a bunk. I was once working on a film and, on one particularly stressful afternoon, for about an hour and a half, I truly believed that I had lost all of Sylvester Stallone's luggage. I seriously contemplated just getting on the Tube and disappearing into another life. That sounds ridiculous now and, of course, it was ridiculous then, but stress can do that to a person. Something less ridiculous? Well, that would be when my loving but dysfunctional parents were simply not holding it together and seemed determined to destroy one another as they expressed their own terrible pain. But even if you feel frightened and small, you have to take a deep breath and get on with it. And if you can find your Courage as you do that, it transforms the situation because then you are being courageous and not simply the victim of circumstance.

The key thing is to remember that Courage is not the same as not being afraid. That's just 'not being afraid'. Courage is the strength you find inside yourself to act even when you are terrified. I once accidently uncovered an act of wrongdoing against a good friend. I could have said nothing, and it would have been a lot easier all round, but my conscience would not rest. So I found my Courage and did what I like to believe was the right thing. It caused huge amounts of fuss, but my Courage held up. As will yours.

As Goethe put it, so succinctly, 'Be bold, and mighty forces shall come to your aid.' And he was right. Courage is transformative. Next time you are afraid, take a deep breath and try it.

HUMOUR

'If you want to make God laugh, tell him your plans.'
Woody Allen

HUMOUR

I realise it's only a few pages since I wrote about laughter, and it's possibly a little early to be rehashing anything. In my defence, however, I think it's true that this one could just as easily be titled 'bad parenting' as Humour, and unlike every other post so far, this one is also about a single specific incident, an anecdote involving Charlie.

So why use this story? There are two reasons.

The first is that it perfectly demonstrates the 'gap' which must exist in order for Humour to be experienced. Humour is created when two opposing ideas are juxtaposed or contrasted and the 'gap' between them is forced shut, creating an emotional outburst that we generally experience as laughter, or Humour. The great northern UK comedians such as Alan Bennett and the late Victoria Wood knew that a great gag can easily be generated when you juxtapose the profound with the absurd. There's a brilliant Victoria Wood sketch where she asks Julie Walters's character if her mother likes Spain. 'Well, she likes the majesty and grandeur of the landscape,' comes the response, 'but she's not too keen on the bacon.'

That's the gap, and whether you find it funny or not is only about whether you relate to it. Make it culturally relevant to your audience – and get the timing right – and you will bring the house down. But even if you have no desire to make others laugh, being able to recognise the gap will help you to appreciate many truly great moments of comedy in everyday life.

Why is it important to be able to recognise the comedy of life? Try hanging out with someone who has no sense of Humour for twenty minutes, as that will demonstrate the answer better than anything I can write here. I've given this a lot of thought over the years and I think Humour is the most effective form of stress management going. Every time you laugh you release a burst of energy that dissipates into the atmosphere as joy, leaving you feeling lighter, happier and less stressed. And stress is a big part of modern life. Everyone has stress of some kind to contend with in their lives, it happens to all of us. Anyone who commutes to work in a big city knows about stress. As does anyone who has ever had to deal with unsolicited sales calls at home. But turning the humdrum everyday stresses of life into Humour is a way to overcome them, and to avoid losing ourselves in them. It elevates our daily round and gives us a commonality with our fellow man. It makes the boring bits of life that bit more bearable. Life can be tough and sometimes we get worn down and forget about important things, like being happy. That's where Humour can help, and if you pay attention, you will realise that everyday life can be an absolute pantomime.

The second reason for learning to recognise the comedy of life is that you will be able to store up a harvest of wonderful memories for your old age: every word of what follows is true and it will keep me chuckling warmly on many a long winter's night into my dotage.

The summer of 2007 was spectacularly wet in the UK. I had gone to pick up Charlie, then aged ten, from a sleepover and en route home I picked up a friend of Esme's who would have been about six at the time. For the purposes of this story and to mitigate the risk of litigation, we'll call the friend Jane.

Lamenting the incredibly wet summer we were having, I asked Jane if she had been away on holiday.

'Oh yes,' she replied enthusiastically. 'We went to stay with friends of Daddy's in France.'

'How lovely!' I replied. 'Whereabouts?'

'A place called Condom,' she said innocently.

Beside me in the front seat, the ten-year-old boy sat up attentively, like a Jack Russell which thinks it may have just seen a rabbit in the undergrowth. Not sure there's anything there but definitely worth further inspection.

'Leave it alone,' I muttered threateningly. 'It's a place in France. Step away from the innuendo.'

Charlie shrugged diffidently and sank back in his seat. I sighed inwardly and decided to change the subject.

'Do you like reading, Jane? Esme is loving her books.'

'Oh yes!' she enthused. 'I really love Paddington, but Mummy just gave me a new book about some children called *The Famous Five* and I am really enjoying it.'

Too late, I watched in dismay as the Jack Russell shot off after the rabbit.

'Oh I loved *The Famous Five*, too, Jane!' Charlie smiled wickedly. 'Now remind me, what were they called? Julian, Anne, George, and the dog was called Timmy . . . who were the others?'

'Dick and Aunt Fanny!' Jane smiled innocently.

'That's right!' cried Charlie. 'Now tell me, Jane, do you think Dick is Aunt Fanny's favourite?'

I wept with laughter for the rest of the journey. God forgive me, it may be bad parenting but it's also Humour.

INTEGRITY

'Don't ever regret being honest. Period.'
Taylor Swift

INTEGRITY

Integrity is not a word you hear a lot these days, not naked and raw like that, but in my perpetual state of glass-half-full optimism, I choose to believe that that is not because it's as dead as the dodo, but simply because we now tend to refer to it by other names.

The dictionary defines Integrity as 'the quality of being honest and having strong moral principles'. If you cast around there are plenty of people you know who exhibit this quality by the bucketful. Think of Harry Potter! I strongly believe that most people possess it; it's just a question of whether or not they have the courage to use it.

Integrity is clearly also that thing the media pundits rant on about all the time, mainly in connection with the behaviour of bankers getting paid bonuses, MPs claiming expenses, huge multinational companies not paying tax, and so on. They don't always call it Integrity, but rant on about it they definitely do, as they most definitely should. Because although those rants are typically lamenting a lack of Integrity, as something more honoured in the breach than the observance, as the saying goes, it's clearly still important to a lot of people. And that is really good news. If there is any hope for humanity, perhaps it lies in the fact that deep down we all still care about doing the right thing.

Those last four words of that sentence are key: 'doing the right thing'. The main point about Integrity is that it's ultimately all about your behaviour. A good friend once said to me, 'You are not what you think; you are not what you say; you are what you do.'

I suppose that the real issue is that, if your thoughts and your words don't match up with your actions, then you run the risk of being described as someone who lacks Integrity. So might we redefine Integrity as 'the alignment of honest principles through thoughts, words and actions'? That definition would certainly allow for such an adherence to high principle.

Marcus Aurelius (Roman Emperor, AD 161–180, the last of the Five Good Emperors, and also considered one of the most important Stoic philosophers) said this: 'Live a good life. If there are gods and they are just, then they will not care how devout you have been, but will welcome you based on the virtues you have lived by. If there are gods, but unjust, then you should not want to worship them. If there are no gods, then you will be gone, but will have lived a noble life that will live on in the memories of your loved ones.'

That seems right to me. If you always do what you think is right, you will never have to worry about anyone finding out, or wondering if you could have done better.

So, how will you know what is right?

Well, I guess we've either done that job by now or we haven't, but I think you guys have all found your moral compasses. You know the values by which we have raised you and by which we would like to think you will try to live. So even if people disagree with you, you will know that you acted with Integrity. They might not like your motives, they might dispute your rationale, but they won't be able to dispute your Integrity.

The bottom line is that people may doubt what you say but they will always believe what you do.

Or, to give the last word back to Marcus Aurelius, who coined it so much more elegantly: 'Waste no more time arguing about what a good man should be. Be one.'

THE 10TH OF 50 THINGS

PERSISTENCE

'Never, never, never give in.'
Winston Churchill

PERSISTENCE

I had a touch of writer's block, sort of lost my 'oomph' for a bit with this one, and was beginning to think that I'd run out of steam. Which got me rather neatly to thinking about motivation and commitment, and also Persistence.

Persistence is defined as 'the fact of continuing in an opinion or course of action in spite of difficulty or opposition'.

So that told me and my missing 'oomph', which was quite useful really because I wrote this in draft form and then managed to delete it and am now having to rewrite from memory as I didn't save it. Yet another useful lesson in Persistence.

I suppose we learn about Persistence when we are babies. When we take our first clumsy step as a toddler, we inevitably fall over quite quickly. But we get up and we have another go. We don't sit there and say, 'Well, it's obviously not my thing.' We keep going at it, don't we? Like Esme learning to play the piano and working out that even a few minutes' practice a day can make a huge difference. And it did, didn't it? We all watched in pride and amazement as she sang 'Somewhere Only We Know' at the school music competition and accompanied herself on the piano.

So Persistence is a useful skill to acquire early, but it's one which, as we get older and life becomes more complex, can get forgotten. If I'm honest, it can feel boring to have to keep applying effort to something that is not paying any dividends. When studying, for example, it's so much easier to focus on the subjects that we enjoy, the ones that come easily to us. But that's when Persistence is key. Devoting more time to the difficult subjects – I'm thinking maths, physics and chemistry here, guys! – will pay dividends in the long term. It's sometimes tough to find the focus or the inspiration, and it's when those qualities are in short supply that Persistence sees us through.

As you know, I've been developing a film project for nearly a decade now. I have frequently felt like giving up. I have marvelled at my own stupidity in persisting, but my problem is that I told all of you I was going to do it. So there is no stopping. Not just because I'm worried you'll never believe me again, but because as well as telling you, I made a deal with myself. So I plod on and guess what, I'm going to do it. Watch me.

It's natural to want to succeed quickly, to want to achieve the maximum possible results in the shortest possible time, whatever the endeavour in which we are engaged. It's also natural to curse our mistakes and setbacks.

As I have become older, however, I've begun to see that the mistakes and setbacks in my own life generally served a purpose to which I was oblivious when they occurred, but the lessons that they taught me have inevitably made me grateful for them later.

Of course, as I've demonstrated, choosing a career in the film industry seems to mean that Persistence had better be a big part of your DNA – in any creative endeavour there are delays and problems, and the film industry seems to magnify these – but I suspect that that is also true for any career. Everyone's journey is composed of single steps and Persistence is the quality that makes you just keep putting one foot in front of another. Literally.

I remember when your grandma, Molly, came to stay after a major operation. For the first week or so she just lay on the couch and I seriously thought she might die under our roof. And then one day, as I sat in my study, I heard the front door go. Looking out of the window I saw Grandma dragging herself along at a snail's pace, using the paddock fence to support herself as she progressed down the drive to the gate, and then back again. It was seriously difficult for her but I wasn't surprised.

You see, your grandma lived through the Second World War and she grew up listening to Winston Churchill. Giving in was never an option.

ENTHUSIASM

'He taught me that if you are interested in something, no matter what it is, go at it at full speed ahead. Embrace it with both arms, hug it, love it and above all become passionate about it. Lukewarm is no good. Hot is no good either. White hot and passionate is the only thing to be.'

Roald Dahl, *My Uncle Oswald*

ENTHUSIASM

I cannot be over-enthusiastic enough about the importance of Enthusiasm. Like all important things, sometimes it's tough to hold on to; in fact, sometimes it's really difficult to find. Part of the problem is that it's probably not very cool these days. If your aim in life is to be cool, then an attitude of casual indifference is so much more fitting than the eager enjoyment that goes with being enthusiastic. I mean, 'eager enjoyment'? You're almost begging to be laughed at. And let's face it, in life, if you want to fit in and win the acceptance of your peer group then it's very hard to go wrong if you just stick with good old-fashioned cynicism.

'Why bother?' can be a really strong question to overcome. And indeed, it's my observation that a lot of people hide in this place. I mean, there are benefits to this. After all, if you never bother, you can never be wrong. Right?

Well, maybe, but I would venture, wrong! Cynicism is just fear dressed up by sarcasm and trying to appear much cleverer that it really is. Sure, it can be incredibly witty, and it can deflate a great idea like a pin popping a balloon. But is a big, fat, diffident nothing really the best thing you can achieve?

When you are faced with fear, with cynicism, you have to smash it. You have to overcome it, you have to dump the cynicism and find your Enthusiasm, even if you have to slap it on like sunblock.

Why? Because nothing happens without Enthusiasm. Work can be hard or dull at times, even in a job you love. Boredom can strike. You can get bogged down in crap that holds up your progress.

But, like its identical twin brother persistence, Enthusiasm is a vital part of your journey to fulfilment, and it will see you through the tough days where work feels exactly like a four-letter word. Enthusiasm will give you fortitude to keep going, and it will build your character into something amazing and compelling. So stick with it.

The etymology of Enthusiasm is from the Greek 'entheos' and can be translated as 'divinely inspired' or 'possessed by God'. So that's something for your cynicism to think about.

I've always told you that the most valuable thing you can do every day is to pay attention to the task at hand And do it as well as you can, with a good attitude. Just do that and you will personify Enthusiasm. Smile when you meet people. Show interest in their activities, as well as your own. Be enthusiastic!

The effect you'll have on the world around you will amaze you!

Firstly, you will change the energy in the room in a very positive way. But you will also transform other people. It takes very little Enthusiasm to dissolve other people's cynicism. See, deep down, they really want to believe. They've just forgotten how. But you can use your Enthusiasm to transform their lack of faith and get them back on track. Think of that scene at the end of *Elf* when they are in Central Park and the only way to get Father Christmas's sleigh to fly again is for the crowds of New

Yorkers to put aside their mighty, collective cynicism and sing 'Santa Claus is Coming to Town'. It's like that, though possibly without the flying reindeer.

Seriously, I urge you to try it – do you remember when we were on holiday and got caught in the rainstorm? We were all wetter than an otter's pocket and a bit dejected because the manager of the hotel told us they couldn't dry anything before we had to leave. So we stood on the rock outside our room and danced in the rain, singing loudly and playing the air guitar and simply celebrating the whole ridiculous episode! Our collective Enthusiasm transformed that whole day into a wonderful memory, which still makes me smile when I think about it. We turned wet luggage into a life-affirming experience. Enthusiasm did that.

FRIENDSHIP

'One loyal friend is worth 10,000 relatives.'
Euripides

FRIENDSHIP

In *Harry Potter and the Philosopher's Stone*, J.K. Rowling writes, 'There are some things you can't share without ending up liking each other, and knocking out a twelve-foot mountain troll is one of them.'

As you all know, I'm a big Harry Potter fan, and I can only imagine that knocking out a troll is a very bonding experience.

I don't mean to be disrespectful to relatives, mine or Harry Potter's, but I do think that Euripides was absolutely right and I've been thinking about why that should be. I think it is to do with the fact that while we are given our family when we get here, our friends are the people we choose to walk beside us on our life path. They are the people we can trust with our pain, the people who have our backs, the people who are not afraid to tell us the truth. We can rely on them totally, no matter the circumstances in which we find ourselves.

And before you ask, yes, of course we should be able to expect those things from our relatives, but for lots of reasons it doesn't always work out that way.

It's kind of amazing when you think about it, because you never know the most significant moments of your life have just occurred . . . You might be excited to meet someone but you don't know that you have just met your best friend; only time can reveal that to you, for it is only over time you realise that's who they are, as they reveal their true self to you, day by day, with every word they speak and with every action that they take.

In my own life, I have been so blessed with friends that when I think of them, of the love and encouragement that they have given me, my eyes get wet. Look at my Friendship with your mum, for example (before she became a relative!), or with your godparents – OK, we lost touch with a couple along the way but most of them are treasured friends! It is overwhelming that someone who has no obligation (through being related) to me should so freely support me, share my life's most important moments, rejoice in my rejoicing and weep tears for my sadness.

So as you might expect, I can't let this go by without paying tribute to my friends, the people who have shared this journey with me, the people who have supported me and loved me no matter how difficult their own lives.

My oldest best friend is Andrew. We met when we were fourteen. We went to different schools, had different interests and came from different backgrounds. Yet here we are, nearly forty years later. We have a bond that has been one of the most important in my life. Andrew knows everything there is to know about me, is unfailingly honest with me and I trust him totally. Why are we such great friends? I have no idea, except that we never fail to make one another laugh. Part of that is down to having a similar (puerile) sense of humour and part of it is down to shared (funny) experiences.

When Andrew and I were sixteen and had finished our

GCSEs, we were allowed to go on a camping trip to Guernsey. These days teenagers go to Ibiza, apparently, but Guernsey was our lot. That's the Dark Ages for you. Anyway, we had a fairly dull week on what is, after all, a small island measuring approximately nine miles long by three miles wide. In those days it was a bit like Bognor Regis, except that you had to go on a boat to get there. By the end of the second day we had cycled all over it twice, and were fast in danger of becoming bored witless as we tried to make our money last the week. By the Friday, nearly deranged with lack of excitement, we splashed out some money on water-skiing. You paid the bloke with the boat your money and he pulled you around the bay three times. Andrew went first, full of confidence, as he had water-skied a lot and was sure he would be very good. However, after only two goes around the bay the boat pulled in. Andrew asked about his third go around the bay, only to be told that his first go counted as two as he had fallen over. Fairly unimpressed with this, we argued but the man told us, in fairly frank Anglo-Saxon, to go away, which we did. We climbed the steps up on to the harbour wall, grumbling fiercely as the boat pulled away with another hapless punter hanging off the back. But as we got to the top of the steps, Andrew smiled and said, 'Do as I do.'

With that, he began waving at the boatman and shouting. When the boat turned and the man saw us, we then turned and mooned at him. What we didn't anticipate was that the man would gun the engines for the shore and begin charging up the steps after us. We belted for our lives, slightly hampered by the fact that we were coughing up our lungs laughing, as well as carrying bikes up a steep cliff staircase. Still, we were young and fit and he didn't catch us and we laughed continuously for days.

And I know that that story is not profound, and is really rather silly, but it's a 'troll-catcher' and I'm proud of it.

My other oldest best friend is Big Charlie (so named to distinguish him from my newborn son, named after him). He has a great analogy for Friendship. He says that if you were going 'over the top' in the First World War, you would let your real friends stand anywhere they wanted, beside you, behind you, in front of you, while those whom you doubted and did not trust, well, you would want them where you could see them. I have adopted that measure for myself. I count my friends as the people who could stand anywhere and I would feel safe. They are the people who would literally have my back and I would feel protected rather than vulnerable. And through the unswerving steadfastness of his Friendship, I would happily allow Charlie the privilege of standing wherever he wants, as I know he would me. And in that cohort with Andrew and Charlie, of course I would have counted Guy, and Steve who inspired this book, and Michael, and Dave, and darling Danielle and Ian, and Emma and Edward, and many, many others.

When I drill down into it, I realise that these people, my friends, are the people with whom I can laugh, with whom I can cry and laugh again. We are bonded, I think, by our courageous defiance against the absurdity of life in which we join together and laugh. Even in our grief, we find something to laugh about together. And no explanations are required.

And the glorious, beautiful paradox is that, if you hang around them long enough, your friends will become your family.

Seriously. Take a look around the room. Those people you are laughing around with right now. Sooner or later you are going to be one another's best men or bridesmaids, then godparents to one another's children, and maybe one of them will even make the leap to being your spouse. So even family starts out with the blessing of Friendship.

I'm giving the last word to A.A. Milne:

'We'll be friends forever, won't we, Pooh?' asked Piglet.

'Even longer,' Pooh answered.

Choose carefully and remember: be the best friend that you can possibly be.

CHARITY

'Is the rich world aware of how four billion of the six billion live?
If we were aware, we would want to help out,
we'd want to get involved.'
Bill Gates

CHARITY

When I was growing up, a phrase I used to hear a lot was, 'Charity begins at home.' It doesn't sound very generous, it sounds like a reason for not doing more than looking after your own, but I like to think it was the understandable reaction of the generation who had lived through the deprivations of the Second World War, not to give away precious resources that might be needed in future. It never sat easily with me, though, and as an adult, whenever Charity has been required, I have always tried to give as much as I felt I could afford at the time.

But as I get older, I have started to question the value of giving money to Charity. After all, it never seems to make any difference. Comic Relief has been raising huge amounts of money for over twenty-five years now, and the problems they are trying to solve grow bigger and more threatening with each successive telethon.

But in a way, if we only equate the value of our giving with the outcome it achieves, we are missing the point. Mother Teresa of Calcutta said, 'It's not how much we give but how much love we put into giving.'

That has to be right. When you were toddlers, if you cut yourselves, your mum and I would put a plaster on your cut and kiss you better. I don't think we ever said, 'It's your own fault, if you hadn't been running it would never have happened.' We didn't measure out our compassion only on those occasions where you were blameless. And so it has to be with Charity, I think. We have to send love as well as money, food, whatever it is, and not judge the success of the venture solely on its outcome.

Let's face it: if judging outcomes is your game, this could get uncomfortable. I used to sit on a committee at Oxfam, and the thing that struck me most over the months I attended those meetings was the realisation that most people who regularly give to Charity do so to a level that they are comfortable with, rather than at a level which is likely to make any real or lasting change in the life of, say, a starving child in the developing world. To a certain extent the charities themselves are to blame for this. They tell us exactly how much it will take to feed a child for one month, and so we fill out the form for that amount and carry on with our lives. (Of course the flip side is that if they told us we all needed to sell our cars and houses and donate the money to them, no one would do it.)

But as a parent I find it tragic that we are prepared to let that be enough: that we don't aspire for that starving child what we aspire for our own children: that they not merely survive, but that they thrive and have an education, a nice home, all the things that we aspire to have for ourselves and our own children. We give enough so that we don't have to feel guilty.

I'm not saying we should necessarily change this, or bankrupt ourselves, but I do think we can do more. We can act more meaningfully without donating more than we can afford.

At this time the world is facing a humanitarian crisis on a scale not seen since the Exodus. I'm talking, of course, about the Syrian refugees, people so desperate that they are prepared to walk their children over mountains in winter, or put them to sea in makeshift boats, rather than risk staying in their own homes. While we debate whether we're having a holiday this year, they are dying for want of our help. So what can we do? What have I done? I've sent money, I've signed petitions and supported campaigns. Sometimes it feels useless and maybe it is, but right now it's the best I can do. If you're doing that, that's all anyone can ask.

On one Sunday morning in the 1950s, your Grandmother Molly attended church as usual. During his sermon, the vicar announced that some Romanian refugees had arrived in the parish and needed somewhere to stay for a few days. Your grandmother came home with a married couple and their baby, and the husband's mother. They stayed for two years. Your grandfather's thoughts on the matter are not recorded, but given the length of their stay, I can't imagine he was terribly exercised by his unexpected houseguests. That is an amazing act of Charity.

Mother Teresa also said, 'Charity and love are the same – with charity you give love, so don't just give money, but reach out your hand instead.'

And that's the crux of it. Sure, give money if that is all you can do, but more than that, if you can, volunteer to help a Charity. Give your time, give your energy, give your love. You won't know what a difference you can make until you try, but if you don't do anything, the outcome will be . . . well, nothing.

In the lottery of life, we are all winners, so please, always do what you can. As children you have all shown me how generous and loving you can be – Charlie giving all his old football kit to the boys who had nothing; Amelia packing Christmas shoeboxes for orphans; Esme sending her hair to be made into a wig for a child recovering from chemotherapy. You've all inspired me, but just remember, as life gets busier and more crowded, it's more important than ever to care for those who cannot care for themselves.

Yes, Charity begins at home, but we mustn't let it stop there.

THE 14TH OF 50 THINGS

SEX

'Having sex is like bridge. If you don't have a good partner,
you'd better have a good hand.'

Woody Allen

SEX

Uh-oh, S. E. X. Awkward.

I have to admit this has been the hardest one to write. Because this isn't about the birds and bees, or the facts of life, as people used to say when I was a boy.

I deliberately put this off for a while, not least because it just felt more than a little uncomfortable, but also because I hadn't worked out exactly what it is I have to say to you about this. I think I've got it sorted out now. If you are old enough to talk like adults, you're old enough to hear what I have to say, so, with a couple of caveats, I'm ready to give it a go.

The first caveat is that I assume you have as much technical knowledge on the subject as you need right now, and that you have worked out your own moral compass, i.e. you know what you think is wrong and what is right and you are steering your behaviour accordingly. The second caveat is that if you ever want to ask me anything you are welcome to do so. I promise not to snigger.

So that said, this is what I have to say about Sex.

Whatever you want to do, provided that it is legal, consensual and unlikely to result in death or injury, is fine with me. As your parent my primary concern is your well-being and happiness, and whichever label you find yourself lining up behind is fine with me. (Actually, I find the labels disturbing because they are so limiting, but I understand why people like them. But please remember that the most interesting thing about a person is never going to be their sexual preference.)

Now when I say that whatever you do, provided it is legal, etc., is fine with me, I am not even going to attempt to address extreme behaviour because I'm assuming that's not who I am talking to (and I appreciate that even that assumption is fraught with difficulty but it's the best I can do right now!). I would like to think that your mother and I have brought you up to love and respect other people. So that when it comes to making love, I hope you will try to have experiences that are meaningful and positive for you and your partner. As the old expression goes, 'whatever two consenting adults do in private' must be fine.

The key word there is 'private', everyone's Sex life should be private. I mention this obvious fact because yours is the first generation to be born into the Age of Information, the first generation to grow up with the world wide web at your fingertips. And amazing though that undoubtedly is, there are times when I yearn for the gentler, less immediate age in which I grew up, when people had more time to make mistakes without being found out, where acts committed out of naivety were not immediately scrutinised by an unforgiving world and subjected to comment and ridicule by cynics and idiots.

You see, to the jaundiced eye of a fifty-something father of teenagers, the internet looks like a pretty unforgiving beast. There is a famous quote by the Duke of Wellington which says, 'Publish and be damned.' The thing is, that expression can work two ways and I would say, when it comes to your Sex life, if you publish, you may well be damned. It follows you everywhere.

Future employers will discriminate against people who have had colourful life experiences and been so indiscreet as to put them on Facebook or YouTube. I can hear someone in the background saying something about people getting famous through Sex tapes and I can't argue with that, but I would say this: is that really what you want to be known for?

Sex is a magical, mysterious, wonderful thing. It needs privacy to flourish. Put a spotlight on it and it may suddenly look rather sordid and ugly.

So as they say in cinemas these days, 'Make sure your phone is turned off.'

It is, after all, a truth universal, that discretion is the better part of valour.

OPTIMISM

'*Choose to be optimistic. It feels better.*'
His Holiness the Dalai Lama

OPTIMISM

Optimism might be described as hopefulness and confidence about the future. It's a great place to live, but it's one of those things that is frequently mocked by people of the pessimistic persuasion. Optimists are frequently accused of being out of touch, of not appreciating how bad things are. I guess I can understand that: after all, it must be so much easier if you assume the worst and behave accordingly. For one thing, you never have to try and, for another, you will rarely be proved wrong.

An optimist must be an idiot to lay it all on the line and assume everything is going to work out just fine.

Right?

Well maybe. Or not.

Speaking for myself, I have to go with Optimism because, even if I am deluded and just plain wrong, it just feels better to think that things are going to work out for the best. To assume the worst is just draining and depressing, and I want neither hand, act, nor part of it.

More eloquently, the American philosopher Noam Chomsky says, 'Optimism is a strategy for making a better future. Because unless you believe that the future can be better, you are unlikely to step up and take responsibility for making it so.' The take-home message here is that regardless of which operating software you run, both are likely to be self-fulfilling prophecies. Which means what?

Well, it means that if you aim low, the chances are you may miss and not be surprised or bothered. While if you aim high . . .? Well, you might fail, or you might succeed. But if you do fail at the first try, you might learn enough to succeed at the next attempt.

So I think you have to discard pessimism because, frankly, it's just not a helpful position to adopt if you are trying to move things along. Also, even if things are going down the drain faster than I can stop them, I would rather hold out hope that a miracle might occur than simply give up and assume it's all a disaster.

In his autobiography, *Long Walk to Freedom*, Nelson Mandela said:

> I am fundamentally an optimist. Whether that comes from nature or nurture, I cannot say. Part of being an optimist is keeping one's head pointed towards the sun, one's feet moving forward. There were many dark moments when my faith in humanity was sorely tested, but I would not and could not give myself up to despair. That way lay defeat and death.

No prizes, then, for guessing that I'm with Mr Mandela on this. If he could do it, so can we. But while I cannot compare my life experiences with those of Mandela, I can well remember your late grandmother, as a single parent of three children, struggling to pay the bills and to keep things going, and yet she always retained her Optimism. Of course there were dark times, every life has those, but my mother used to say, 'If the Lord doesn't come, He sends,' and somehow, He always did.

I don't know anyone who doesn't face challenges. It doesn't matter if you are trying to get elected, writing a book, trying to be a great parent/husband/wife/sibling, or simply giving up caffeine, each of us is faced with challenges to overcome on a daily basis. You've all had to take school exams – I recall that the revision was a bit of a challenge? As for me, I promise to try harder with the caffeine next time. But be clear about this: it's Optimism that gives us the courage to try!

So I'll give the last word to Winston Churchill who said, 'For myself I am an optimist – it does not seem to be much use to be anything else.'

Chin up!

THE 16TH OF 50 THINGS

CHOICE

*'I am fine with whatever choices you make,
as long as you are happy to live with the consequences.'*
Dad

CHOICE

Choice, or choosing, is a bit like breathing: it's something we do countless times each day and yet most of the time we are unaware we are doing it. And, like breathing, it's also vital to our day-to-day existence. Just as the quality of the air we breathe can make all the difference to our health and well-being, the same is true of the quality of the choices we make.

The trouble is that some of our choices seem so small and trivial on the day we make them that it's hard to imagine that they will have any consequences down the line. So we tend to ignore the potential backdraught and carry on regardless.

As you might expect, the level of consequence really does depend on the Choice in question. If the Choice is about whether to have raspberry jam or peanut butter on your toast, it's probably not that life-changing. But if the Choice you are making is to smoke your first cigarette, that might lead to a second and third cigarette, and that might lead to a lifetime smoking habit. I've seen lung cancer close-up; it's not pretty.

Goethe said it more eloquently: 'Choose well. Your choice is brief, and yet endless.'

Now, I hope I have made it clear that the point of this book is not for me to lecture you about how to live your life. It's about putting down markers for you that will hopefully help you to make your own decisions, your own choices.

And the thing I really want you to take on board about Choice is that in every moment of your life, whether you care to acknowledge it or not, you are making choices. Even if your Choice is to not make a Choice, or to allow someone else to make the Choice, it's all Choice. And every Choice has a consequence.

So as your parent, I'm going to reiterate one key point:

I am fine with whatever choices you make as long as you are happy to live with the consequences.

I'm not going to tell you not to do anything, although I absolutely reserve the right to debate with you if you involve me beforehand.

And, obviously, I would prefer you to make good choices that don't hurt you or anyone else, but my own experience has taught me that life is not always neat and tidy. In fact, if I am sure of anything it is that you have to make mistakes to learn anything of value. For example, I am sometimes asked to write project pitches for prospective clients. I used to do it. But on one or two occasions, now, I have handed over a considerable amount of free work outlining a marketing strategy for a particular project, and then not been hired. So, my mistake, and I have learned: I don't do it any more. If my body of work or my current clients are not enough to persuade people that I may know what I'm doing, I'm probably not the right guy for them anyway. So out of the mistake of making a stupid Choice, I've hopefully made a smart Choice.

You also have to bear in mind that as you get older and the choices get bigger, so some of the consequences may get bigger too. There may be consequences your mum and I can't bail you out of. For example, if you decide not to bother revising for any exams, the results may not be what you might have wished. Similarly, if you take a pill offered to you in a nightclub by a fascinating stranger, well, we may not have a cure if it turns out not to be what they said it was.

I know it won't always be possible to think before you make a Choice, but even being aware of that fact is better than not even knowing that you are making a Choice.

My lovely friend Phil took a job in Australia. It was a big decision – he had a wife and young children and it meant uprooting everyone from their lives here, away from the support network of close family and friends, and taking them thousands of miles away. I asked him why they decided to go. He replied, 'We decided to go when we realised that not going was as big a Choice as going.'

So, be aware. Try to make good choices. Remember that in certain circumstances you can probably have the raspberry jam *and* the peanut butter. And also remember that, wherever possible, I will always support the choices you make.

HEROISM

'A hero is someone who has given his or her life to
something bigger than oneself.'
Joseph Campbell

HEROISM

After some indecision, I have decided to write about Heroism. Yesterday was the massacre at the offices of *Charlie Hebdo* in Paris, and I say indecision because, after these tragic events, it was hard to know if democracy or freedom of speech might be just as apposite. But some of the commentaries I've heard this morning, in which some people have suggested that we should voluntarily restrict our freedoms to avoid offending others, have got me thinking.

After all, as Ursula Le Guin once said, 'Nobody who says, "I told you so" has ever been, or will ever be, a hero.'

So, as I say, this one is about Heroism, as a tribute to the journalists who died yesterday, exercising their democratic right to freedom of speech, and to the policeman who died trying to defend them.

First of all, Heroism is defined, quite simply and elegantly, as 'great bravery'.

On that note, let me say this: according to the news reports, when the gunmen stormed the *Charlie Hebdo* offices on the morning of 7 January 2015, they called out the names of the cartoonists who had most offended them, and those men, who must surely have known that they were about to die, bravely met their fate. The magazine's publisher, Stéphane 'Charb'

Charbonnier was among them. He had previously been quoted as repeating Euripides' phrase 'I would rather die on my feet than live on my knees', but he and his colleagues who were slain alongside him were no less heroic for their pragmatic view of their own bravery.

Similarly, the policeman who had already been wounded and tried to confront the gunman must have known he was going to be killed, yet he still tried to prevent the terrible attack. That's Heroism.

As you know, *Charlie Hebdo* had upset terrorists before. In 2006, their offices were firebombed after they published a cartoon that was deemed offensive. At that time, the late Christopher Hitchens said, 'There can be no negotiation under duress or under the threat of blackmail and assassination. And civil society means that free expression trumps the emotions of anyone to whom free expression might be inconvenient.' Amen to that.

Why do I care so much? I've already written about tolerance, so I won't rehash that, but what we are encountering here is an ideology which says, 'If you offend me, I have the right to kill you.' At one level that's just a toddler who needs a smack on the bottom; at another it's psychopathic or fundamental barbarism; back when I was a lad, and political parlance was not the bad joke it is nowadays, we used to call it fascism.

You won't remember the fascists but you have learned about them. Back in the 1930s they started a thing going in Germany. No one was too worried to start with because they were simply too ludicrous to be taken seriously, but they pandered to people's fears and suddenly they were in power. That's when the trouble started. We called it the Second World War. I'm deliberately being frivolous to make the point here. No one took them seriously, but they started off by burning books that offended them, and by the end they were burning the people they didn't like, the people whose race or religion offended them.

So at this point, just as I want you to remember what those people in Paris actually died for, it also seems appropriate to remember what Winston Churchill had to say: 'We shall never surrender.'

But what do I mean by that? Well, simply this: now, more than any ever, it is absolutely vital that we all satirise together whenever we wish it, whenever we choose. This is important so that you can develop a healthy world view, one in which you can see that not all Muslims are a threat to your way of life, any more than you are to theirs.

I would never expect or encourage you to behave in a way that was disrespectful to another person's beliefs (tolerance and courtesy, remember!), but we must defend these little freedoms – such as democracy, the rule of law, freedom of speech – with all our strength, for they are hard-won, God-given rights, and no man can be allowed to take them from us, even if your very life is under threat.

So it's simple. We have to stand and be brave. We have to exercise our right to a free life under a benign democracy, because if we don't, it will be taken from us. We can't allow that because too many good people have died for those beliefs for us to let them down now.

Remember the people in Paris.

Je suis Charlie.

THE 18TH OF 50 THINGS

GOSSIP

'The more you know, the less the better.'
Billy Connolly's granny

GOSSIP

Gossip is a tough one. It can feel like so much fun at the start. You can tell by people's body language when they have something juicy to tell you. They hush their voice and lean forward to create an atmosphere of secrecy. You're being invited to join an exclusive club. How exciting! Plus, this is privileged information and you are about to hear something great! And now, thanks to the world wide web, Gossip comes in lots of different formats – on Twitter, on Facebook, it's everywhere, on every platform so far invented. And with the way technology is moving, this is only the beginning.

The thing is, by the time the gossiper in front of you has whetted your appetite, you're probably past caring if any of it is true. It's just so much fun! Because, let's face it, no one ever gossips about people's great virtues or good works. People only Gossip about other people's bad behaviour or problems.

When I was a child I heard a lot of Gossip, mostly sitting pretending to do my homework while my mother and her friends talked about other people, also supposed to be their friends. It always struck me as odd that they would talk about their friends that way. How would they feel if people talked about them like that? The weird thing was, that never seemed to occur to them.

It was only as I got older that I started to realise that Gossip is actually really nasty. It's corrosive, like the worst kind of poison, and it attacks people's reputations. Sadly, an untruth spoken often enough and left unchallenged becomes history, just like the nastiest tabloid headline that assumes that everyone acted out of the worst motives as it calls down judgement. And just as the tabloid newspaper headline is presented as entertainment, so it is with Gossip when, in reality – and I mean this absolutely – it is nothing more than the celebration of human suffering.

To be clear: I'm not talking about the kind of conversation in which people catch up with one another about their lives. I'm not talking about shared family histories or news about other people's children, or how great it was to attend a wedding or a party. I'm talking about negative chatter about people who are not there to put their side of the story. We all know the difference.

Think about it: when someone tells you that so-and-so has split up with whatsisname and the drama that went on between them, that's already a tragedy in those people's lives. Never mind that it isn't anyone else's business; never mind that no one else alive has the right to an opinion on the matter; never mind that no one outside of so-and-so and whatsisname can possibly know what *really* happened: the wilful celebration of others' misery demeans us all.

So by now you're probably getting that I'm not a big fan of Gossip.

You are right. It's toxic. Leave it alone.

Instead, try to remember this: everyone is doing the best they can according to what they know. If they knew better, they would do better. If they have screwed up some aspect of their private life, they are in great company because sometime, somehow, we all do it. So don't be too quick to jump on the bandwagon, but if you do have to take a position on the matter, remember that in the same way that a good journalist can twist the most innocent of soundbites to make it fit the agenda of his story, so Gossip can twist facts and hearsay into the most poisonous conjecture. (Actually, with a heavy heart I have to admit that a bad journalist would be just as adept at this kind of wordcraft, but you get the point: it's part of a storyteller's stock-in-trade. As they say in advertising, 'Don't sell the sausage. Sell the sizzle.') If you are hearing something from someone other than the person who did it or to whom it happened, then you are probably not hearing the full truth but a mangled version of it that bears some, but not enough, resemblance to what really happened.

I urge you to remember that, in case you are ever unfortunate enough to hear something that someone has said about you. Especially if the person alleged to have made the remark is one of your best friends. (Trust me, it happens.) My advice is this: if you didn't hear it said, if you don't know exactly what the context of it was, then give the person the benefit of the doubt.

For as Alexandre Dumas wrote in *The Three Musketeers*, 'There is no friendship that cares about an overheard secret.'

Trust me on this: take a deep breath, be noble and rise above it. You will save a ton of energy and your friends, your real friends, will know that you are a person of grace and integrity.

And *that*, I think, is worth talking about.

GRATITUDE

'Gratitude is not only the greatest of virtues,
but the parent of all others.'
Cicero

GRATITUDE

Gratitude is the apple-a-day of virtues. Quite simply, like making choices, it is as important as breathing. Never expressing it would be like never taking a deep breath. And just as never taking a deep breath would mean you'd never experience the sense of well-being that comes with taking bracing lungfuls of fresh air, so never expressing Gratitude would mean that there was no celebration of any aspect of your life.

And that would be tragic because, when you think about it, there is so much for which we should be grateful, every single day.

There is a fantastically funny passage in Bill Bryson's wonderful homage to the UK, *Notes from a Small Island*, in which he writes about all the great reasons we have to be grateful, for never being unhappy. You should read it, but especially the chapter on Weston-super-Mare. As he points out, when you consider that the sperm that conceived you had to beat off competition from approximately 25 million others, just being here, reading this, is pretty much a miracle for which you should be grateful.

And if you start with being grateful for just being alive today, what else is there that you could genuinely celebrate? Your health? The love of your family and friends? Your dogs? Having enough to eat? Living in a secure democracy? Having access to a loo that flushes and clean running water? There really are myriad things to be thankful for in every moment.

Now, I realise that this may fast be turning into one of the most annoying things you've ever read. I don't mean it to; and I realise that it sits rather oddly in today's media culture which tends to focus our attention on all we do not have rather than what we do.

So let me just say now that I understand and accept that there is nothing more annoying than someone like me being all 'Pollyanna' about everything if what you really want to do is sulk and rant at the world. (And by the way, it's fine to rant and sulk occasionally; sometimes it's really good to vent before you take that deep breath and move on. Just don't let it go on too long. Five minutes should be enough.)

The good news is that this chapter will still be waiting for you when you are ready to remember that there really is so much for which to be grateful.

As I have alluded to above, Gratitude is one of those things that's sometimes more honoured in the breach than the observance; it's something you maybe notice most when you don't do it. I mean, try not breathing and see how that works out for you. Likewise, never expressing Gratitude can get stale pretty quickly. But similarly, like the smallest of muscles, if you exercise it regularly, you'll be amazed how quickly it can grow. If you've ever had to fetch water from a well, you'd learn to be grateful for a mains supply pretty quickly. (Personally, I always silently bless the dishwasher as I turn it on.)

What I am trying to say is that even on your worst day there will be things you can be thankful for, things you can find that will assuage the pain or the grief you are going through. After watching my mother's last months of life, months during which she was racked with pain and distress, I was so grateful to witness her die in peace, free of pain. I never thought I would be grateful for something like that. Conversely, when Amelia was born a rather alarming dark blue colour and did not breathe properly for rather longer than we all would have liked, I was so immensely grateful when she finally decided to join the human race and take her first gulping breath.

That is something for which I have never stopped being grateful, just as I have been grateful to be the father of all of you, each and every single day of your lives.

I remember the day that Charlie found Amelia's doll ('Spanish Baby') hidden in his toy wheelbarrow behind the door in the hall. Amelia was so touchingly grateful to her big brother, while Mum and I were both grateful that she never questioned how her doll got stuffed into the space behind the door in the first place. (Anything you'd like to tell us, Charlie?)

In *Winnie-the-Pooh*, A.A. Milne wrote, 'Piglet noticed that even though he had a very small heart, it could hold rather a large amount of gratitude.'

Like Piglet, you will be amazed at how much your heart can hold. It's just a question of saying thank you!

HAPPINESS

'You will never be happy if you continue to search
for what happiness consists of.'
Albert Camus

HAPPINESS

I nearly wrote the title in capitals: HAPPINESS!!!! Because, let's face it, Happiness is today's 'Must Have' emotional accessory. Furthermore, if you take a brief look around our marketing-driven world, it's pretty clear that the entitlement to instant, profound and life-changing happiness forevermore is top of everyone's list. Whether it's a new car, the latest version of the FIFA game, a night out with the Kardashians or the holiday of a lifetime, the message is that you are going to feel really happy once you have it. After all, what could be more important than your right to Happiness? Nothing, right? That's right! And nothing can be allowed to stop you doing whatever it is you feel you need to do in order to be HAPPY!!

Except . . . hmm . . . really? As your father, I'm not so sure. I think I'm pretty much prepared to sacrifice anything I need to in order to protect and nurture you guys. Certainly Happiness would be the first thing to get tossed out of the basket. Because I couldn't be happy if you guys were not safe and well. And guess what: I'm not unhappy about that. That's what I signed up for when I became a parent. Ask anyone who has children. Ask anyone who loves someone else more than they love themselves. The truth is that you guys are actually my Happiness, personified as Charlie, Amelia and Esme Dunne of Titley, England. There you go, walking around all over the place, outside my head, doing stuff and freaking me out the whole time. But I guess we're all getting a kick out of that. I know I am. In fact, it makes me happy.

In reality, though, the direct pursuit of Happiness is like chasing your own shadow. It's elusive, tiring, frustrating and, most importantly of all, no one has ever caught it that way.

If you want it in a nutshell, here it is: in my experience, real Happiness is best found in the pursuit of other things. The thing is that Happiness, in and of itself, is not something you can simply acquire. It's a by-product. Trust me when I tell you that I am as certain as I can be that real Happiness is never found when it is your sole purpose. In fact, the fastest way to become seriously unhappy is to focus on yourself and what you think you need to achieve your right to lasting Happiness.

Happiness is kind of like a unicorn: much sought after but never seen, except fleetingly, at dusk, in a magical place. So, if you want to be happy, go and find that magical place: do something that turns your attention outwards and take in all that the world has to offer. As you apply yourself to that task or activity, something like contentment will strike you, and as you continue Happiness will arise from deep within you. Yes, that's right. It's already there. You just have to let it bubble up.

And one way to achieve it really quickly is this: go and do something for someone else, to make them happy, and without hope or expectation of any reward or recognition. Give that homeless person ten pounds. Volunteer to visit the elderly. Help someone without being asked. Perform an unwitnessed good deed or a random act of kindness. Be a force for good in the world and seek nothing in return. When you throw away your internal balance sheet, Happiness will flood into your life and you will be a blessing to everyone who knows you.

And of course, as I write that, I recognise that blissful state of being is an ideal to be aspired to, and that if you're feeling a bit hacked off with life, this could actually make you feel quite grumpy and want to go into the corner and say rude words.

That's fine. I get it. But as Hamlet advised his mother, 'Assume a virtue, if you have it not.' So when you have finished sulking, put on a big smile and remember: just because you can't catch your own shadow, doesn't mean you shouldn't dance with it!

RELIGION

'Anyone who thinks sitting in church can make you a Christian must also think that sitting in a garage can make you a car.'
Garrison Keillor

RELIGION

I have to say, I thought the one about sex would be tricky but, in our modern world, Religion is a tough gig.

It's tough because there is so much to say that you might misinterpret. And I really don't want to appear disrespectful of anyone else's beliefs. But, on the other hand, what the hell!

It's no mystery to any of you that I believe in God and that to a certain extent I am a Christian. I say 'to a certain extent' because I feel that I am only observant to a point, but I was brought up in the Church of England and I am comfortable with its traditions. I sometimes think it is slightly obsessive about sin, but there you go, no one's perfect. (Which is kind of the point, right? If I wasn't a miserable sinner I wouldn't have anything to talk about.) There are some Christians who might question my daily practice of Transcendental Meditation, and I'm fine with that. The point is that, as a model or guide for living your life in a way that causes the least amount of harm possible, Christianity is perhaps not the worst path a man might tread. Before anyone mentions the Crusades, I'm clearly not talking about religious and cultural imperialism, but rather 'Love thy neighbour as thyself'. Actually, as commandments go that's a nice one to have to follow. Certainly it's hard to argue that the world would not be a better place if we all did it. But the thing I really love about Christianity is that, actually, sinners really are welcome. In fact, it's pretty much the mission statement: Sinners welcome. Everyone is redeemable. We don't give up on anyone.

But similarly, over the years I have also come to see that practising Christianity is not the same as being Christian. If you look around, there is no denying that there are a lot of people talking the talk but then doing nasty things while masquerading as the good guys; even worse, there are people doing seriously wicked things in the name of Religion. I was going to say that's bad, but actually it's more than that: it's evil.

But when cynicism strikes and you are tempted to write off Religion for all time on account of that evil, here's the thing you have to remember: there is no Religion in the world that does not have love as its core message. Not one of them is based on violence and evil. So when people tell you that the Catholic Church supports child abuse, or that Islam is a Religion of violence, I'm afraid they are as deluded as the people committing those acts.

Of course, the problem is that people are fallible. We all fail at some point. Our own fallibility is in letting theirs become the overriding message and drowning out the love.

When I was a child, in my Anglo-Irish half-Protestant-half-Catholic world (I told you I was mixed race!), I was very well aware that my French Catholic and Irish Catholic cousins viewed us with something akin to disdain, even pity. Of course, the French Catholics also viewed the Irish Catholics with total scorn and disdain, but I was too young to appreciate the comedy of that back then. But us non-Catholics? Well, we were definitely not going to inherit the Kingdom of God because that was reserved exclusively for them. In fact, the local Catholic priest once declined to bless us when he called at the Irish cousins' house, prompting my mother to remind him of Christ's words, 'Suffer little children to come unto me.' But then, honestly! I mean, that guy Jesus, what did he know about Christianity? Bloody do-gooder.

That kind of nonsense, falsehoods masquerading as truth – and our acceptance of the same – goes on all the time, and not just in Religion. (Wait until I get on to Politics!) But that doesn't mean that you have to buy into it, and nor should you let it interfere with your relationship with God, whatever that looks like for you.

At the time of writing, Charlie is an atheist, and Amelia and Esme have both been confirmed. And all of that is great.

I rather love what Mahatma Gandhi said: 'God has no religion.' And so I guess if there is anything to take home from this, it's that, for me, it is more important to love God than it is to practise a particular Religion. All roads lead to Rome, after all.

And if you all happen to end up residing in that happy state of certainty known as atheism, well good for you. As C.S. Lewis said, 'A man can no more diminish God's glory by refusing to worship Him than a lunatic can put out the sun by scribbling the word "darkness" on the walls of his cell.'

Above all else, remember this: God loves you, and so do I.

RESPECT

*'Respect is one of life's greatest treasures. I mean,
what does it all add up to if you don't have that?'*
Marilyn Monroe

RESPECT

Respect is sometimes defined as 'due regard for the feelings, wishes, or rights of others'. And sometimes it is defined as 'a feeling of deep admiration for someone or something elicited by their abilities, qualities, or achievements'.

So that's Respect then. Ask Aretha Franklin, she'll tell you.

However, there is also a timeless aphorism about Respect which says that it has to be earned rather than given; commanded rather than demanded. And this is where it starts to get tricky. It's tricky because Respect is a quality, which, if we don't have it for ourselves, is hard to cultivate for anyone else.

For that reason alone, it seems to me, Respect (like integrity) is more noticeable when it is absent, which is to say: a lot of people forget about Respect completely in their dealings with the wider world. Sadly, it's no great mystery when that happens; it's pretty self-evident in everything they say and everything they do.

So if people continually behave with a total lack of Respect for others, how do we improve things? Well, the good news is that, in certain circumstances, such as when there is a deficit of Respect, it only takes one person to change the world.

So here's what you do: you have to give Respect. And I think you pretty much have to give it unconditionally.

In Charles Kingsley's classic children's tale *The Water Babies*, there is a character called Mrs Doasyouwouldbedoneby. (She has a colleague called Mrs Bedonebyasyoudid but for now we'll stick with Mrs Doasyouwouldbedoneby. Still with me? Good!)

Now what was great about Mrs Doasyouwouldbedoneby was that she was true to her name, and by her words and actions she personified not only unconditional love but also Respect. After all, if we always treat others as we ourselves would like to be treated, it's unlikely we are going to tread on many toes.

And how we behave towards others has an undeniable effect on the way they behave towards us as well as to others. Some people take longer to learn than others, so you may not change people overnight, but, more importantly, that shouldn't be your aim.

It's called 'paying it forward'. It's about ignoring other people's lack of Respect for themselves or anyone else and respecting them any way you can. And yes, I realise that it may not always be easy.

I can remember once being in Dublin visiting my father. As we were walking through town in the middle of the day we saw a man who was clearly beyond acceptable levels of drunkenness, who was deranged with anger and emotional pain. As he flailed around in the street, roaring incoherently at invisible demons and random passers-by alike, a man began grappling with him in a futile effort to bring him under control. The more disturbing thing was the second man's evident hatred. He spewed out bile that was even worse than the drunkard's, because it was coherent. His vicious dismissal of the man's life as worthless was incredibly sad to hear. As we walked away, your grandfather said quietly, 'Always remember: every man is some mother's rearings.' It's a very elegant way of saying that, simply by virtue of his humanity, every man is worthy of your Respect.

And that's it, really. Everyone is worthy of your Respect, whomever they may be.

If you can manage that, Mrs Doasyouwouldbedoneby would be proud of you, as, indeed, I am every day.

DIGNITY

'I don't want to be remembered as the girl who was shot.
I want to be remembered as the girl who stood up.'

Malala Yousafzai

DIGNITY

Dignity is the tweed jacket of virtues. It's not sexy, it's definitely not fashionable, and if you wear it to a summer picnic people will probably laugh at you. But when storm clouds gather and things get rough, it will protect you from the cold wind and rain and, deep down, everyone else will be staring at you and wishing that they had one just like it. (I probably should have said I meant an English summer picnic.)

But just as an English summer picnic demands blankets and waterproofs, so there is an ambiguity to Dignity that makes it hard to define. Somehow, though, everyone seems to have a sense of what it means and, more especially, of what it means to be denied it.

The *Oxford Dictionary* defines Dignity as 'the state or quality of being worthy of honour or respect'. To our modern sensibilities that definition has a fairly antiquated feel to it, a bit like an Agatha Christie film set in the 1930s when everyone spoke with cut-glass accents and no one ever complained in public. It's already starting to feel like something of an anachronism in the modern age.

And yet . . .

Aristotle said, 'The ideal man bears the accidents of life with dignity and grace, making the best of circumstances.'

Did you see what I did there? I was trying to find a quote that would illustrate the relevance of Dignity to modern life so I quoted Aristotle who died in 322 BC. Luckily for me, Aristotle was a genius whose philosophies are as relevant today as they were in ancient Greece – they can take a bit of untangling but it's well worth the effort – but in a way, the fact that the most relevant thing I could find was said so long ago illustrates perfectly not only how tricky a concept it is to grasp, but also how timeless it is.

I think what Aristotle is saying is that Dignity goes hand in hand with having a bit of backbone, being phlegmatic about awkward circumstances, bearing the tough times with equanimity and not complaining. You can make wry observations, witticisms, social commentaries even, but never complain. In fact, I can tell you from personal experience that complaining is one of the surest and fastest way to lose friends. (The other way is to block a septic tank but we need not go into that just now.)

Aristotle also said, 'Dignity consists not in possessing honours, but in the consciousness that we deserve them.'

That suggests a quiet confidence, a self-assuredness, a modesty if you will, that doesn't let itself get rattled by other people or their opinions of us. It's not a demanding energy this one, but rather a quiet strength that gently emanates from deep within us, giving reassurance both to us and those around us who are calm enough to recognise it.

I'd love to tell you that I could name countless forebears who demonstrated this personal Dignity, but I think it bypassed my family, or maybe they just confused it with coldness. Maybe that's why I'm such a big fan, especially when I see the three of you demonstrating it without even knowing that is what you are doing.

I had a funny brush with Dignity last year. I was staying at a hotel in London and had just gone back to my room, funnily enough to fetch my (tweed) jacket, when Mum called me: the dogs had caught a wood pigeon. Senior black Labrador, Syd, had taken possession of it, while the other three were trying to get it from him. As a fight looked imminent Mum tried to get it from him but he wouldn't let go. Now, as he is a highly trained dog – but *my* dog – Mum thought that if I shouted down the phone, he might let it go. As you know, I am always game for a laugh so I put on my sternest 'dog obedience' voice and shouted, 'Sydney! Release! Release, Sydney!' Sydney cocked his head and stared at the phone but did not relax his grip on the pigeon and eventually, after several minutes of shouting 'Release!', Mum and I gave it up as a bad job.

All fine, until I opened the door of my room to find a chambermaid poised with key card in hand, looking absolutely stunned. As I walked past her with as breezy a 'Good morning' as I could muster, I saw her look cautiously around the door, as though expecting to find someone tied to the bed. And with that I pushed my chest out, my shoulders back, and strapped my Dignity into place. What else could I do?!

It's good to be frivolous to make a point but there is another Dignity, of course, and that is the Dignity we talk about in the negative sense. That is, in the sense that someone has been denied their Dignity, or their Dignity has been violated. We hear this particularly in reference to people who have been subject to violence or rape.

Appalling as those things are, I would urge you to remember that even though someone may violate your Dignity, they can never take it from you. Look at Malala Yousafzai whose

Dignity carried her through an appalling ordeal to become the youngest-ever winner of the Nobel Peace Prize.

So, stand tall, shoulders back, and don your invisible tweed jacket. Others will envy you, even if your dog ignores every word you say!

ACCEPTANCE

*'Acceptance doesn't mean resignation; it means
understanding that something is what it is and that there's
got to be a way through it.'*
Michael J. Fox

ACCEPTANCE

Acceptance reminds me of the story of *Alice's Adventures in Wonderland*, when Alice is at the Mad Hatter's Tea Party. The Mad Hatter instructs Alice to serve the cake, so Alice tries to cut the cake before she serves it. Only that won't work and the Mad Hatter tells her to serve it first and then cut it, which works brilliantly!

Bear with me: I'm not going mad, or at least I don't think I am.

Now, according to Wikipedia, 'Acceptance in human psychology is a person's assent to the reality of a situation, recognizing a process or condition (often a negative or uncomfortable situation) without attempting to change it or protest.'

All well and good. However, it goes on to say that Acceptance is a core dogma of most world religions, which makes you think there must be something to it.

When I was in my teens, many of my school holidays were spent in Ireland with my father and his second wife, Nuala. They were both recovering alcoholics and, from the age of about eleven, I was used to hearing this prayer whenever I stayed with them:

God grant me the serenity to accept the things I cannot change,

The courage to change the things I can;
And the wisdom to know the difference.

It's called the Serenity Prayer and it's pretty well known by recovering addicts everywhere. I think my dad and Nuala used it whenever daily life threw challenges at them which, in their drinking days, they would have dealt with by consuming dangerous amounts of alcohol. Having chosen a better way to live, they now recited the Serenity Prayer to get them through tough moments when life seemed not to be going their way.

And that's really the point. They didn't feel serene when they said it; right then in the moment they were really struggling to accept what had just happened. My point is, it was not an easy place for them to get to.

So they said the prayer, repeatedly, and as they did so the ritual of the words somehow comforted and calmed them and helped them to regain their equilibrium without recourse to booze.

In other words, they had to shine it on, to reverse engineer it, as Alice had to do with the Mad Hatter's cake. (Now do you get it?) In the same way that the cake had to be served before it was cut, so their Acceptance had to be assumed before it could be felt. And sometimes it was as tricky as the cake.

The point of all of this is really simple: in life you are going to be faced with many situations that you do not like and which you may feel you are powerless to change. If you can learn to accept them, you will get through them so much more easily. You can spend a lifetime resenting what did not go your way or you can accept it and move on.

Here is a case in point from our own home life. When Esme was about three years old, our refrigerator gave up the ghost and we had to replace it. Esme must have been at playgroup or somewhere like that when it happened, because later that day she came into the kitchen and said, 'Where's the fridge?'

'It's there,' I said, 'There's the fridge.'

'Not that fridge,' she said, eyeing me beadily. 'Where's *our* fridge?'

'That's our fridge.'

'Where's our old fridge?'

'It's gone. That's our new fridge.'

And somehow, in that moment, I knew that Esme was not OK with this, that our casual replacement of a major piece of her landscape was not a trifling matter. A point proven some three weeks later, when she wandered back into the kitchen and blithely announced, 'I'm fine with the new fridge now.' It took some time but, finally, Acceptance prevailed.

I'll finish with a happier quote from a master of English story-telling, H.E. Bates. In *A Little of What You Fancy*, the second of his chronicles about the Larkin family, Bates wrote: 'The quick and high degree of her intelligence that lay under the languid, golden surface of her wit and patter was one of the things that had first drawn and then endeared her to the Larkin philosophy: namely, that life was sweeter, fuller and richer if you went with the stream, rather than tore your heart out rowing against it.'

As someone who has wasted many hours trying to row against the stream, I can promise you that if go with the flow, practise Acceptance, you really will have a much better time of it.

THE 25TH OF 50 THINGS

INNOCENCE

'*Innocence is a kind of insanity.*'
Graham Greene, *The Quiet American*

INNOCENCE

Innocence is one of those things that is practically never mentioned until it is lost or abused; only then does it seem to warrant a mention. I used to think that was bad, but over time I have realised it's a good thing, because it means that Innocence is assumed to be a natural state of being, or, as you guys would say, a default setting. I love that. (Of course, I should make the point that I am writing about Innocence as a virtue and not as a legal term of reference, though even in a court of law it is a state of being which, we are assured, is assumed until proven otherwise.)

As if to illustrate that point about its observation being a sin of omission, my habitual trawl through the usual sources for meaningful quotes has delivered barely anything about Innocence that was not completely subjective. Nothing really helped to pin it down.

Ernest Hemingway, ever grumpy, said: 'All things truly wicked start from Innocence.' Thanks for that.

For all I know, he's right, but I would like to think that if that's the rule, there may be some exceptions.

The thing is, it's so hard for adults to be anything other than cynical about virtues like Innocence, and I think that is because we encounter so much easy cynicism in daily life. But sometimes, life changes you: when you fall in love, when you have children, somehow it all changes as you begin to discover the world anew through fresh, unjaundiced, uncynical eyes; innocent eyes which perceive Creation as the miracle it is, before the pressures of life and its responsibilities crowd in. Innocence then, in those halcyon times, is something to be protected and cherished, in a way that is at odds with the realities of modern life.

I used to wonder why we tell little children about Santa Claus and the Tooth Fairy and the Easter Bunny and so on. Why do it? Well, now that I am a parent of teenagers I know that we do it for two reasons: firstly, in order to preserve the Innocence of our children; and secondly, to recapture our own. Think about it: as a four-year-old, you are the master of the known universe. Whatever you want, you get. If you don't get it, you yell until you get it. And all you know is that if you are willing to keep yelling, eventually you will win.

So now, approach it from a parent's point of view. We're all trying to raise nice children, who understand boundaries and who know that when we say 'No', we mean exactly that. We also want you to be people who are kind and appreciative and full of wonder at the miracle of the life you are discovering fresh each day. The lessons of love and appreciation learned through the imparting of small miracles, like the Tooth Fairy leaving a coin beneath your pillow as you sleep, are never forgotten. And even as we get older and stop losing teeth, the lessons remain with us.

I've given it a lot of thought and I think it comes down to this: if you thought it was your parents leaving you a Christmas stocking full of gifts or leaving money under your pillow in return for your discarded teeth or casting chocolate eggs around the garden, well, it's just possible that your four-year-old self's natural appetite for more-more-more might overrun the innate good manners we are trying to draw out of you; it might destroy your moral fibre, you might succumb to avarice. So we tell you about Santa & Co. in order that you know and appreciate what a special thing it is that someone, especially a semi-divine being with supernatural abilities, should go to the trouble of bringing you a gift of any kind. To preserve your purity of heart and to keep you in your Innocence.

One of the greatest filmmakers the world has ever seen, Federico Fellini, had this to say: 'No matter what happens, always keep your childhood innocence. It's the most important thing.'

I'm with him. When my darling god-daughter Hannah was four, she was very happy to have a devoted godfather and I quickly became the font of all useful knowledge in the universe. For Hannah's doting parents, this was charming at first, but over time it became a little grating when every time they pondered a question aloud it was answered by the shrill certainty of a toddler saying, 'I'll ask Peter. He'll know.' To their credit, however, even that held good until the day the family car broke down. Sitting in the back of the car on her booster seat as they awaited the recovery vehicle, Hannah asked her mother what was wrong with the car.

'I don't know, darling.'

'Never mind,' Hannah said. 'I'll ask Peter. He'll know.'

At which point, her mother replied in some fairly frank Anglo-Saxon which would have left her daughter in no doubt whatsoever about my mechanical abilities. Some Innocence lost? Perhaps. But a good life lesson nonetheless.

THE 26TH OF 50 THINGS

HONESTY

'The truth just sounds different, doesn't it?'
Cameron Crowe, *Almost Famous*

HONESTY

If I'm Honest right now, this feels a bit late in the day. I mean, at this point this lesson has either been learned or it hasn't, but, on the other hand, I remind myself that this whole exercise is to serve as a reminder to you, should you ever need it.

Good old Shakespeare coined that universally used aphorism: 'Honesty is the best policy.'

I'm curious that he didn't tell us why. I guess it's supposed to be self-evident, and I guess the good news is that it pretty much is, right?

But lying can sometimes – OK, often – look like a great way out of a sticky situation, even though anyone with a hint of decency about them must cringe at the idea that it's OK to brazenly mislead people so that we can get our own way. I do remember feeling mortified when Esme realised we had lied to her about the Tooth Fairy, unleashing a devastating cry of 'YOU LIED!!!', but that's my cross to bear. I stand by my argument on innocence.

As it is, most lies aren't that clever and the truth generally gets uncovered sooner or later, and embarrassment, not to say punishment, generally ensues. If you think about the moral indignation and outrage inspired in tabloid newspapers by stories about lies people have told, while it can sometime feel like a bit of an overreaction, it does also tell us that there is still a really high premium on Honesty. It must be really important if newspaper proprietors can still sell papers on the back of it.

I can't think of a lie I've ever told that was worth it, even counting the fact that there were some that I felt compelled to tell to protect other people, if not myself.

The point is that Honesty demands courage because sometimes Honesty will cause more trouble than a quick lie. But that trouble is generally only avoided in the short term, a fact the dissident Soviet author Aleksandr Solzhenitsyn knew well when he wrote: 'The simple step of a courageous individual is not to take part in the lie. One word of truth outweighs the world.' Solzhenitsyn was exiled to a gulag in Siberia for being Honest, so he was well qualified to make that observation.

But what I've also learned is that the people who make a fuss when you tell the truth are generally those people who are not familiar with it. Think about it: who would prefer a lie except a liar? And the more fearlessly you practise your Honesty, the more courageous you become until, *Honestly*, you just don't think about it any more.

Over the thirty-odd years of my career, I've worked with several dozen senior executives who were very influential in the companies in which they worked. The ones who stand out, the ones whom I respect even more than I like and admire (and by the way, they are the same ones), the ones I would follow over hot coals in bare feet, are the ones who fearlessly told the truth regardless of the cost. They are the people for whom Honesty was an uncompromising operating software that could not be corrupted. They were the Simon Cowells of my world, and if I earned their praise I knew it was genuine. There was no easy lie to flatter me or to make me feel secure and indebted to them.

Conversely, the people who lied fluently, and cared nothing for their own reputation or those of others, would have sold snake oil to blind people. While in my youth I may have fallen for their charms, I soon learned to steer away from them if they hadn't already thrown me under a metaphorical bus to cover up another lie.

In life, many people will tell you what you want to hear, especially if you are paying them or if they want you to do something for them. But it takes real courage for people to tell the truth to their employers, those in authority who might be able to punish them, those whom they love who might reject them. Flattery is SO much easier.

But you have to go with Honesty because, well, you just do.

The morning after my mother died, your Auntie Sarah phoned me to talk about the funeral arrangements. While we were talking she mentioned that Millie, who was then three, had told her she had dreamed of our mother that night, and that Grandma had kissed her and told her she loved her and then disappeared. It was very touching and both Auntie Sarah and I wept as she related it.

Later that day, I was at Auntie Sarah's house to meet with the funeral director, and Millie wandered into the room, dragging a dolly behind her.

'Hi, Millie,' I said. Millie smiled at me.

Auntie Sarah said, 'Tell Uncle Peter about Grandma.'

At that point, Millie clearly thought that no one had yet told me the bad news, as she looked me straight in the eye and said, 'Your mother's dead.'

The great thing is that, even as we were weeping with laughter, we all knew how wonderful Millie's Honesty was. I'm pleased to say it's an attribute Millie has retained into adulthood and I commend her for that because it's not always easy.

As the Austrian philosopher Ludwig Wittgenstein said, 'Nothing is so difficult as not deceiving oneself.' And if you struggle at times with the charm of liars, just try to recognise Honesty when you hear it.

The good news is that, if you listen closely, it really does sound different.

THE 27TH OF 50 THINGS

HOPE

*'Hope is being able to see that there is light
despite all of the darkness.'*
Archbishop Desmond Tutu

HOPE

Hopefully – do you see what I did there? – Hope is like an old T-shirt that you wear all the time without thinking about it. Sometimes you might forget to put it on, but when you do it just slides into place as though it's never been away. It's not smart or sexy, it's not going to win you many awards, and some people who are too afraid to drop their guard might mock you for it, but somehow, in spite of all of that, it is a huge comfort.

While holed up in an Amsterdam attic, her Jewish teenager's view of life limited to a small skylight looking up to a world riven apart by the Second World War and the horrors of the Holocaust, Anne Frank, a fourteen-year-old Dutch girl, wrote in her diary, 'It's really a wonder that I haven't dropped all my ideals, because they seem so absurd and impossible to carry out. Yet I keep them, because in spite of everything, I still believe that people are really good at heart.'

So, having taken a moment to pause with wonder at those remarkable words of Hope written in the least hopeful of circumstances, always remember that if Anne Frank can do it, so can we.

Friedrich Nietzsche wasn't having any of it. He said, 'Hope in reality is the worst of all evils because it prolongs the torments of man.'

Which may or may not be right; I guess history decides, but frankly it's too sodding gloomy for me. I need to believe that things can always be better. And if Anne Frank could hold on to it, Nietzsche can get stuffed.

At one point in John Carpenter's 1984 film, *Starman*, Jeff Bridges' character says that what he finds beautiful about the human race is that 'you are at your very best when things are at their worst'.

That's Hope, right there. Don't you dare give up on it.

Looking back, I realise that I was a pretty neurotic child, and growing up I was prone to worrying about things other people seemed to ignore. To be fair, I think I had good reason to be neurotic. By the time I was ten my parents were divorced and our family life felt very unstable; I was a child who craved structure and yet my overriding fear and concern was that my mother appeared to be overwhelmed for much of the time; in the wider world the country was being torn apart by trade union strikes – we had winters of endless power cuts – and, in addition, I was just old enough to realise that we were in a nuclear arms race with the Soviet Union. My world felt very unsafe and, honestly, the terrors of my imagination knew no bounds. The possibility that a siren might announce we had four minutes until we were blown up felt very real to me, and I prayed constantly that calmer heads would prevail and we might live in peace.

One day, I confided in a family friend who listened to my fears; she didn't patronise me and tell me not to worry, though she did say that she thought we'd be OK, and then she quoted Julian of Norwich: 'All shall be well, and all shall be well, and all manner of things shall be well.' It's a quote I have loved ever since and, actually, what I love about it is its simplicity. It's not grandiose and analytical; but in the grace of her language, Julian of Norwich cuts through everything and reveals a universal truth. And whether my prayers or Julian's words made any difference, I don't know, but somehow we managed to wangle our way out of an arms race that looked certain to end in obliteration. So I guess I was not alone in hoping for a better outcome. All I know is that my Hope helped me feel better.

Going from my rather pedestrian experience to the amazingly profound: Desmond Tutu's quote at the top of this chapter is remarkably powerful, coming from someone who lived through the fight against apartheid under a vicious South African regime. I heard him speak a few years ago, and it was incredible to hear him describe how every new dawn brought more news of overnight disappearances and murders of his brothers and sisters in arms. The fact that he could even think about Hope is a miracle. He related that at the height of the struggle he got a letter from a woman in San Francisco telling him that she got up at 2 a.m. every night to pray for him. I guess a man without Hope or faith might have dismissed her as a nutcase, but brave, hopeful man that he is, Tutu exclaimed, 'People are getting up to pray for us at two o'clock in the morning! The apartheid regime doesn't stand a chance!' He never gave up Hope, and nor should you.

If nothing else, the fact that both Desmond Tutu and Anne Frank could hold on to Hope also makes me fervently believe that Hope is the only way forward. Not only for each of us individually, but also for mankind as a race. If you don't believe, if you can't Hope that problems can be overcome, that lives can be enriched, you would have nothing to aim for, nothing to work for and, ultimately, nothing to live for.

So we're back to Hope. It's the only option!

MORALITY

*'Morality is simply the attitude we adopt towards people whom
we personally dislike.'*
Oscar Wilde

MORALITY

Morality is a hoary old chestnut. Case in point: the Oscar Wilde quotation above. But much as I love Wilde I do think there may be more to it than that.

If you look it up, Morality is defined as: 'the principles concerning the distinction between right and wrong or good and bad behaviour', and also as 'a particular system of values and principles of conduct'.

Taken on those terms then it should be fairly straightforward. But again, I think there is more to it.

If you take the second definition there, about 'a system of values and principles of conduct', it starts to get tricky – by which I really mean interesting – right away. At that level Morality is like fashion: ever changing; it means something different to every generation. In Victorian times it was considered immoral for a woman to reveal her ankles, or to ever be alone with a man who was not her husband or another close relation. Today such restrictive standards are the preserve of a handful of religious sects.

Similarly, when I was a child, it was still considered immoral to sleep with someone before you married them, or to have children without being married. And I'm sure there are still people who hold that such behaviour is not moral. Even more recently, we have seen law changes allowing gay couples to marry. Bearing in mind that fifty years ago it was not only regarded as immoral to be gay but also illegal, and you realise how much things have changed.

But the problem with fashion is exactly that it does change according to the seasons, and that changeability, while it might be an honest reflection of the evolving society in which we live, doesn't make for very solid ground on which to base your life and the values by which you wish to live. After all, one man's meat is another man's poison. Against a background of subjectivity like that, how do you reconcile yourself with clashes between the modern world and the culture of your upbringing, the social and religious backgrounds in which one is raised?

It's tricky, because at some point we're all going to find ourselves out of step with the 'Morality of the day'. Either you reject the social mores that were in fashion when you were growing up, or you confront the modern world with an air of outrage. It's tricky and that's why I think we need to take the initial, broader view of Morality: it *has* to refer to the distinction between good and evil, rather than a reinforcement of rudimentary prejudices and reactions based on outdated social values.

My grandmother Elsie was a wise old biddy. She used to say that you should try to live your life in a way that caused no suffering to others. If you think about it, you can almost stop right there. It covers everything. As I have grown older, I have learned that it's not as easy as you might think, but I do think it's a great guiding principle.

I've also come to think that if you really can't avoid making a Morality call, one of the things you have to give great weight to is motivation. What causes someone to act in a particular way? I remember reading a newspaper article about a young woman who was earning her living as a prostitute. The tone of the article was pretty judgemental, but it was clear that her motivation was to feed her young children. What's more noble than being willing to sacrifice yourself for your children? Sure, she was living outside the social convention of the day, but was she evil? Clearly not.

Henry Thoreau, said, 'Do not be too moral. You may cheat yourself out of much life so. Aim above morality. Be not simply good – be good for something.'

Go with that and you won't go far wrong.

THE 29TH OF 50 THINGS

SACRIFICE

'Dulce et decorum est
Pro patria mori.'
Wilfred Owen

SACRIFICE

In 2014 we saw the centenary of the outbreak of the First World War. Almost exactly 100 years ago, armies of young men – young men like you, Charlie – from cities and towns across the country, even tiny villages like ours, were preparing for a battle of unimaginable scale. There was no democratic process for them to decide if they wanted to go to war, but theirs was an age in which the good of the nation was synonymous with the good of its citizens. Off they marched to foreign battlefields where, tragically, many made the ultimate Sacrifice and gave their lives for a greater cause, that of a safer world for their families, for their nation and the wider world as well. Of course, we could debate endlessly whether they should ever have been put into battle in the first place, but at the end of the day, they were. They sacrificed themselves for future generations: i.e. us.

And so it has gone on, on and off, ever since. If you sit in our church on a Sunday morning and let your mind wander during the sermon – something which my mind has no trouble doing – you will notice the memorials to the Gwyer family. They are on the right-hand side between the pulpit and the first stained-glass window. Charles Gwyer died in 1915 at Chunuk Bair, Gallipoli, aged thirty-two. His brother Cyril Gwyer gave his life at St Leger, France, in the August of 1918, less than three months before the

Armistice. And Cyril's son Geoffrey Gwyer died in Tunisia in March 1943. There is something so poignant about this triptych of family plaques, because it tells the story of so many families in this country: two generations of men – brothers, fathers and sons – dying at the same age, all in the service of their country, each one following a common path that led them all to make the same ultimate Sacrifice.

The *Oxford Dictionary* defines Sacrifice as 'the act of giving up something valued for the sake of something else regarded as more important or worthy'. As I alluded to above, it's not a common value these days, but that level of Sacrifice was not unusual for families in this country in the first half of the twentieth century. In fact, in the First World War troops were sent into battle by county, so on any particular day all the young, battle-fit men between the ages of eighteen and forty-two from, say, Herefordshire, went into battle together. If it was Ypres or the Somme, the chances are that they all died together that day. And on that day, that county was widowed, robbed of its men. A hundred years later, thanks to newsfeeds and war memorials, their Sacrifice still feels close and relevant, and is still humbling to think about, even if theirs is not a world we recognise any more. Which is exactly what they sacrificed themselves to give us: the freedom to live without worrying about Sacrifice.

Wherever you end up with the politics of it all, the 'should they, shouldn't they have ever been sent into battle' discussions that go on in the media or in the history classroom, one thing is clear to me: however futile the battle appears with 20:20 hindsight, the act of Sacrifice of our troops ennobles the whole affair. It is a worthier cause because of their Sacrifice, and all the more so because they did not act as the aggressor. They went to protect the vulnerable and to support the weak, i.e. the nations that were being overrun by enemy forces. Never forget that. They went to the aid of people who could not defend themselves.

But what do you do with that? How do you honour it? In these days when warfare is a much more internecine affair, fought by faceless terrorists whose primary aim is to make us cowed and afraid in our own cities, in our own homes? How do you honour the people who die at the hands of faceless terrorists – who are as sacrificed as the men and women who died in other wars?

Here's what I think you have to do.

Firstly, I think you have to wear your poppy with pride. Go online and look at the pictures of the ceramic poppy display at the Tower of London, and let it sink in that every single poppy there represented a life lost in battle. That crimson wave in the moat of the castle represents a generation who gave their lives for our freedom.

And, secondly, I think you have to live your life as fully and as nobly as you can. This is not a rehearsal, this is your time, so shine as brightly as you can and cherish the freedoms for which they fought, and, cheerfully if you can, defy those who would deny them to you.

Their Sacrifice has lasted a hundred years. It will last hundreds more, and as you remember them on every Remembrance Sunday, perhaps send them a silent prayer of thanks for all that they gave up in order that you might live freely today.

CONFIDENCE

'If you're presenting yourself with confidence,
you can pull off pretty much anything.'
Katy Perry

CONFIDENCE

In my opinion, Confidence is the trickiest balancing act going. When it's done right, it's based on an innate modesty that comes from knowing that we know what we're doing; but sometimes, if its foundations are not solid, it can become false and idiotic and there's nothing you can do to hide the smell.

Think of *The X Factor* or *Britain's Got Talent* auditions. We've all watched and admired the people who walk on to the stage, centred and calm, knowing that they can deliver on their promise to the judges. Watching the judges' expressions change as the performance starts is really amazing, no more so than when they heard Susan Boyle sing for the first time. But contrast that performance with many, many others, where the performer has walked on to the stage with, shall we say, a slightly different perception of their talents than the rest of us, perhaps one based on fantasy rather than reality, and you start to get the picture that overblown Confidence can be a cruel and ugly prankster.

Calibrated correctly, though, Confidence is an impenetrable breastplate in a well-worn suit of armour – you simply have to have it strapped on before you set forward on to the battlefield of daily life. Just having it on may make you brave enough for what lies ahead, may encourage you to try when you might once have turned back. And that may be the thing that makes all the difference.

It is definitely true that Confidence is your friend. Confidence becomes that self-fulling prophecy. Just by having it, you change everything. Of course, sometimes you have to pretend a little, or let others inspire you. I remember learning to do a backward dive into the school pool. The first time was awful, I was consumed with nerves and literally had to talk myself up the steps to the board, trying not to look at the water. My swimming teacher was a former Australian Olympian and he said, 'Dunne, I know you can do this. Take a deep breath and go.' And something in his voice made me think, 'If he thinks I can do this, then I can.' So I dived and I wasn't awful at it, either. Of course, after that it just got easier every time.

As my willingness to embrace the risk grew, so did my Confidence. And that's a vital skill for life because, trust me on this, no investor, or anyone else, ever stands behind an innovator or maverick who does not passionately believe in his own idea, and equally in his own ability to fulfil it and achieve success. So it's not enough simply to *be* confident, you have to inspire that same Confidence in those around you. And how do you do that? Easy. By being confident.

Walt Disney said, 'Somehow I can't believe that there are any heights that can't be scaled by a man who knows the secrets of making dreams come true. This special secret, it seems to me, can be summarized in four Cs. They are curiosity, confidence, courage, and constancy, and the greatest of all is confidence. When you believe in a thing, believe in it all the way, implicitly and unquestionably.'

So the big question is this: how do you keep a check on

yourself, how do you stop it tipping over into that overblown Confidence, or worse, arrogance?

The answer to that one is the Eleventh Commandment: 'Thou shalt not kid thyself.'

If you think about it, you know deep down when an idea has merit, or if you are right; you get a deep, instinctive Confidence way down in your belly; but you also know when something stinks and you're trying to keep everyone else from finding out, and that's when you know (if you aren't too afraid to be honest with yourself) that you've lost the plot. At that point you're running on that overblown Confidence or arrogance. Not pretty. You see it a lot in the film business: people know that they have made a stinker of a film but they're too far in to admit it. They kid themselves that if they spray a lot of scent around that no one will smell the corpse; sadly it never works, the audience always finds out. You see it in those trailers where all the best moments in the movie have been packed into two minutes. They want you to think that the movie is packed like that for two hours, but the truth is, you know they have thrown everything in there because they have nothing else. And it's generally true to say that if they had not broken the Eleventh Commandment a long way back in the process, probably at script stage, they wouldn't have such a mess on their hands.

But let's walk back towards the light for a moment. Mahatma Gandhi said:

> Man often becomes what he believes himself to be.
> If I keep on saying to myself that I cannot do a
> certain thing, it is possible that I may end by really
> becoming incapable of doing it. On the contrary, if I

have the belief that I can do it, I shall surely acquire the capacity to do it even if I may not have it at the beginning.

If you think about Gandhi's life for a moment, you have to marvel at the Confidence he must have developed to rise to the position he did, the spiritual leader of India at a time when that nation was striving for its independence from the British Empire. But he was certain of the rightness of his cause and that gave him unassailable Confidence to push on, against the overwhelming odds that he faced.

So, just remember the rules, develop that strong sense of the Eleventh Commandment and be confident!

DEMOCRACY

'*Democracy is worth dying for, because it's the most deeply*
honorable form of government ever devised by man.'
Ronald Reagan

DEMOCRACY

So we live in a Democracy, and thank God for that. Every five years we have a general election and the country goes to the polls to vote for the party we wish to lead the country for the next five years.

They say that people get the government they deserve. I think that is true, but I really want you to think about that as you read this.

The great Aristotle said, 'If liberty and equality, as is thought by some, are chiefly to be found in democracy, they will be best attained when all persons alike share in the government to the utmost.'

From Aristotle, some 2500 years ago, to now. That's how long the idea has been alive; that's what Democracy is supposed to be. All of us taking part, all of us having a voice. Or, as I like to think, something like the last line of Abraham Lincoln's Gettysburg Address: 'that government of the people, by the people, for the people, shall not perish from the earth'. We're supposed to be engaged in this process, guys!

And I'm emphasising that because of a conversation we had over lunch with some of your friends at the time of the 2015 general election. It was clear that none of your generation there present cared a jot about the election or what the result might be.

None of you felt engaged in the way this country is run, or that your views on the matter would ever be relevant. Given how many people have sacrificed their lives over the years to ensure that we might live freely under a democratically elected government, that struck me as a failure. Not of yours, but mine, or rather a collective failure of your parents' generation, to instil in you the importance of Democracy. (I'm slightly mollified that you were not the only young people there who felt that way; and I'm also relieved that the other parents were as horrified as we were.)

The worst of it is that such apathy is almost fashionable. And although that is totally understandable, it is not acceptable. Of course, it's so much easier to be cynical, to believe witty epigrams such as: 'it doesn't matter which party you vote for, because the government still gets in'. It's so much less painful to dismiss a political idea with a clever remark than to watch someone painstakingly nurture a fragile ideology that might just change lives for the better. Who wants to live with all that pain? Apathy is much easier, especially when the government seems to operate like a belligerent nanny in a children's story, restricting treats and rewards until special occasions when promises are made and then broken.

But, actually, you have to rise above all of that, you have to keep remembering Aristotle, because if you believe the social commentators, the media, the politicised celebrities, you might believe that what we have ended up with, in this country at least, is a largely benign dictatorship in which, on one single day in every five years, we, the people, have a chance to change the colour of the prime minister's tie.

I do realise that it isn't a perfect system. Ralph Waldo Emerson said, 'Democracy becomes a government of bullies tempered by editors.' And I think he's right, so thank God for a strong, free press (if only we still had one).

But all of that aside, compared to a lot of places in the world, where petty dictators and tyrants masquerade as democratically elected leaders, I'd say it's still a pretty good system.

So let's stick with Aristotle for a moment longer.

In spite of the horrors promised by the right-wing press, it seems to me that the 2010–15 coalition government was actually a really good example of Democracy. By virtue of the fact that neither party had an outright majority, there was a lot more negotiation about significant policies than there might have been if there had been a clear winner. A coalition of parties, having to work together and compromise on a daily basis in order to keep the country running, isn't that what Aristotle was talking about? Everyone being involved.

Winston Churchill said, in 1938:

> You see these dictators on their pedestals, surrounded by the bayonets of their soldiers and the truncheons of their police . . . yet in their hearts there is unspoken fear. They are afraid of words and thoughts: words spoken abroad, thoughts stirring at home – all the more powerful because forbidden – terrify them. A little mouse of thought appears in the room, and even the mightiest potentates are thrown into panic.

So don't be thrown into panic if Democracy doesn't go your way, if you don't get the result you hoped for. It may sometimes be uncomfortable but if it is, that's the moment to get involved, to decide to take part. It's too easy to complain, so don't. Instead, do something different: take action. Become involved with the party you want to support, act on your beliefs. Take part. Protest. Take ownership of your Democracy. You need to make it up to me for your previous apathy, so I want you to ignite your interest because only by taking part can you effect change. Social action at least gives you a platform from which to express any cynical views, but, without it, you just have no right to be cynical.

In the first free elections in South Africa following the collapse of apartheid, millions of South Africans queued for hours and hours and hours and hours to vote, to exercise the voice which others died to gain for them.

Likewise, remember the suffragettes. It is almost unthinkable that in this country, in the last century, women died fighting for the right to vote, to be emancipated. But when you feel too cynical to be bothered, please remember Emily Davison, the woman who threw herself under the hooves of the King's horse at the Derby in 1913, so that you might have the right to choose whether or not to vote at all.

In times of uncertainty, it's vital to remember that we all have a voice, hard won for us by brave souls who refused to stand down. We owe them our respect and we honour them by voting.

CREATIVITY

'Others have seen what is and asked why.
I have seen what could be and asked why not?'
Pablo Picasso

CREATIVITY

The dictionary defines Creativity as 'the use of imagination or original ideas to create something; inventiveness'.

Frankly, I think that must be the least creative definition of the concept possible. I know it absolutely says what it is, but could it be any drier? Not much to inspire the soaring spirit there. Perhaps the problem is putting it into words, trying to nail it down precisely. Maybe it's one of those things that it's better to talk *around* rather than *about*, to try to define its meaning?

Henri Matisse said, 'Creativity takes courage.'

That feels slightly better to me. It feels like it's at least taking a stab at explaining the concept, and let's face it, it really does take courage.

Imagine J.K. Rowling as a young, single mother, walking to a coffee shop every morning to write her first novel. While I am certain that, like all aspiring novelists, she hoped that one day it might be published, and even successful, she can't possibly have known how successful it would be, or that it would become the bestselling children's book of your generation, or the bestselling children's book ever. My point is that she was flying blind. There must have been days when she wondered what the hell she was doing. Why not give up the dream and get a job that would allow her to provide for herself and her baby daughter? I think it's fair to guess that the answer to that is that anything else would have been much harder than what she was already doing. I think the Creativity that drove her helped her to find the courage to continue, and I know we are glad that she did.

Then think about poor Vincent van Gogh, who was driven mad by his artistry, his innate Creativity. It made it impossible for him to compromise; he had to be an artist. Yet he was never appreciated in his own lifetime, indeed he never even sold a painting, yet now his works sell for hundreds of millions of dollars at auctions all over the world. It's immaterial to him, and heartbreaking to anyone who cares, but my point is: Creativity definitely takes courage.

But it also takes vision.

I once heard Creativity defined as the ability to make connections between previously unconnected objects.

In that literary masterpiece *The Little Prince*, Antoine de Saint-Exupery – do read it again, it's so beautiful! – wrote, 'A rock pile ceases to be a rock pile the moment a single man contemplates it, bearing within him the image of a cathedral.'

So you start to get the picture? Creativity arises from allowing the imagination to flow, in letting thoughts collide in gloriously chaotic ways so that somehow, like atoms bubbling around in the atmosphere, they form bonds with other atoms, and then become molecules that somehow attract more ideas and thoughts and, one day, in a magical, quite mysterious way, they become form and change the world for ever.

How exciting is that? The notion that a thought you have floating around in your head right now might lead you to create something never seen before? Of course, not all thoughts are worth much, but just imagine if you paid attention to the small handful that might just be worth something? After all, what have you got to lose?

I remember Charlie getting a commendation for an English essay in Year 7 when he wrote about sheep grazing in the field at night being 'silver-lit by moonlight'. Beautiful imagery created out of previously unconnected thoughts.

When all of you were little, you would bring home paintings from nursery, great blobby splashes of colour without much form or structure, but they would always have a wonderfully imaginative story behind them that would light up your eyes as you told us all about it. (Your mum reminded me early on never to ask what it was, but rather to ask you to tell me all about it!)

I think there is a hint in all that blobby paint and it's this: if you want to be truly creative, you may have to dare to step outside of boundaries set by social convention. You may have to dare to be different from everyone else.

Well, I would say you are already different from everyone else, so carry on. Embrace who you are and let your Creativity flow from that. Celebrate your differences from everyone else in the world, and find your courage. When you align your courage with vision, you will do extraordinary things.

Think about it: this whole project, *The 50 Things*, started out as an idea Steve gave me as I struggled with becoming fifty and then, astonishingly, became a blog that people in dozens of countries have read. And now, it's a book. That's Creativity!

CHRISTMAS

'My idea of Christmas, whether old-fashioned or modern, is very simple: loving others. Come to think of it, why do we have to wait for Christmas to do that?'

Bob Hope

CHRISTMAS

This one is slightly different – after all, Christmas is an event rather than an emotion or a virtue or principle. But it's generally inescapable for most people I know, and, as you'll see below, in my experience it definitely has the potential to be an emotional juggernaut.

The truth is, things always start to tense up a bit in the build-up to Christmas. A few days before the big day, as expectations rise, so fuses shorten. There may be fireworks! But, generally, Christmas is a really special time of year, not just for our family, but for many families around the world

In my experience it wasn't always so. In fact, when I was growing up, Christmas was dreadful. Such high hopes, such crashing disappointment. Growing up in a dysfunctional family with alcoholic parents and step-parents, I was able to give lengthy, considered analysis to the factors required for a pleasant Christmas.

The first is that you do *not* entertain the erroneous but widely held belief that a woman with average cooking skills, working alone, can use a domestic oven to produce enormous quantities of restaurant-quality food at a moment's notice, while under the influence of enough gin to sink a ship's company and without aid or assistance from other people. It is in defiance of every law of physics ever discovered. I know I say this a lot, but trust me.

The fact that we entertain this notion not just for the feast of Christmas itself, but for all of the mealtimes in the week-long hiatus that now surrounds the festive season, is itself delusional. Our friend Saffron calculated that Christmas with her and Michael's extended family was going to mean she was responsible for 200 meals over a five-day period. That's not Christmas. That's a soup kitchen! Now do you understand why things can get a bit fraught?

The other factor, the other truth you must challenge, is the notion that any piece of cheap crap wrapped in brightly coloured paper and tinsel will transform anyone's life.

Again, trust me: I'm not being pejorative about anyone else's Christmas when I write that. I truly and sincerely believe that everyone is doing their very best according to what they know. But I also realised early on that if I was going to have an ongoing relationship with Christmas, I needed to find something more than all this disappointment; something more than the devastation of realising that, yet again, I had awoken on Christmas Day only to discover that I had not been adopted by Richard Branson or the Queen.

How did I do that? Well it started with giving. Truly, it was that simple. Give. Just give. Give way more than you can reasonably expect to receive. And whatever your expectations are, reduce them. Now reduce them again, halve that figure, subtract its equal and work from there. Zero expectations. You can only go up from here.

It may sound extreme, but what it gave me was a Christmas where I didn't experience that familiar disappointment that our home had not transformed into a Klosters ski chalet complete with real Father Christmas and elf-shaped helpers. And, I suspect, because I gave more of myself in a cheerful and generous kind of way, I was maybe more fun to be around. Perhaps the adults didn't feel such a crashing sense of responsibility and self-blame? I don't know, but it certainly made it easier for me.

But as I grew older, I still marvelled at this obsession with a two-month shopping festival that culminates in a roast meal. Seriously? Many families eat a roast dinner every Sunday, so what was it about Christmas that demanded enhanced levels of familial devotion? Why did everything have to be perfect at Christmas, and was that demand for perfection the problem in the first place?

And the answer to that last bit was 'Yes'. We were focusing on the wrong thing.

Don't get me wrong. I love the experience of Christmas as we celebrate it. I love carols, Christmas pudding, mince pies and Christmas trees, and I love the excitement that builds as we get towards the day itself. I even love Christmas jumpers! But I also now know why it is important to me and it is because of what Christmas represents, the values it upholds, that makes me love it so much.

My favourite Christmas carol is 'It Came Upon The Midnight Clear' by Edmund Sears:

It came upon the midnight clear, that glorious song of old,
From angels bending near the earth, to touch their harps
   of gold:
'Peace on the earth, goodwill to men, from heaven's all-gra-
   cious King.'
The world in solemn stillness lay, to hear the angels sing.

I love the idea that at Christmastime, angels draw near to the earth and sing, that we might hear them. Maybe that's why this is a special time of year? Maybe it is that, whether we know it or not, we are in the midst of a celestial celebration of light and love that is greater than any shopping mall experience you can ever wish for.

We say that Christmas is the season of peace and goodwill towards all men. It's the time of year when we express bonhomie to everyone, and if that bonhomie is sometimes given a bit of a nudge by a glass of mulled wine, so what? What's important is that we express love to one another and that is better than anything you can wrap.

So, for a moment this Christmas, try to give something to someone who has less than you, or more need than you. Try to express that love, that bonhomie, to a stranger in need. Give. Just give.

The thing is, whether you believe in God or not, it's hard to dismiss Jesus. Debate this with me for a moment: this is a man who was allegedly born over 2000 years ago in Palestine. He never wrote a book, never travelled a great distance, never appeared on *Letterman* or *Graham Norton*, never wrote a blog. Yet, over two millennia later, some of us still debate his very existence, while many more of us still celebrate his birth year in, year out. As someone who has spent a career in public relations, I can tell you that it is not possible to manufacture that level of fame for that length of time without having something very solid on which to build. So even if a lot of us are celebrating Christmas by misbehaving at office parties (I mean, who hasn't run off 200 photocopies of their naked bum? Just me then) and running up credit card bills, why bother to do any of that in his name if he meant nothing? It makes me think that the lessons he taught, to love thy neighbour as thyself among them, were of more lasting value than anything else we have seen in our entire civilisation. And maybe that's the take-home message here: the giving is perhaps more important than the gift. What do you think?

The Nobel Laureate Sigrid Undset wrote:

> And when we give each other Christmas gifts in His
> name, let us remember that He has given us the sun
> and the moon and the stars, and the earth with its
> forests and mountains and oceans – and all that lives
> and move upon them. He has given us all green things
> and everything that blossoms and bears fruit and all
> that we quarrel about and all that we have misused –
> and to save us from our foolishness, from all our sins,
> He came down to earth and gave us Himself.

Which, for me, just about wraps it up.
I leave you with this: 'Christ's Nativity' by Henry Vaughan:

> Awake, glad heart! get up and sing!
> It is the birth-day of thy King.
> Awake! awake!
> The Sun doth shake
> Light from his locks, and all the way
> Breathing perfumes, doth spice the day.

And to you three, my best Christmas presents ever, and to all the people kind enough to read this, wherever you are, whatever your beliefs, and whatever Christmas means to you, I hope that all your Christmases are filled with love and joy.

COURTESY

'A tree is known by its fruit; a man by his deeds. A good deed is
never lost; he who sows courtesy reaps friendship, and he who
plants kindness gathers love.'

St Basil

COURTESY

So, here we all are then: random assortments of stardust hurtling through space on a giant mud pie that's orbiting a ball of fire that gives us all our power. If that were not enough to be thinking about we must also contend with the fact that, as we whirl through this space-time vortex on its way to who knows where, we must do so alongside roughly 7 billion other souls, including Kim Kardashian and Donald Trump and some people who like wearing purple. In a crucible of such emotional intensity as this, it is not unknown for grown men to tremble and weep. People have even been reduced to muttering rude words.

So that's why I'm writing this one about Courtesy.

Courtesy is defined thus: 'the showing of politeness in one's attitude and behaviour towards others'.

When you were small, I used to tell you that you could say anything you wanted to me, as long as it was polite. It was a message that took some time to get through, but I know it worked because one day, on the way to school in the car, I was singing along to the *Shrek* soundtrack when Amelia, then aged five, said, 'Daddy, that's very nice, but would you mind singing it in your head?'

I remember feeling very smug that day, thinking that my work was done.

But sometimes a message needs to be reinforced.

The thing is, at times, everything gets heightened. I don't know if it's to do with the changing of the seasons or daylight saving or hormonal imbalances caused by eating too much fried chicken, but everyone seems to wig out a bit occasionally, and it is only right and proper that we should allow them to do so.

As long as we remember some basic rules.

Well, one basic rule, actually.

Courtesy.

St Basil was on to something there. Every man you meet is worthy of your respect. In fact, let me go so far as to say that whatever you achieve in life, were you to become the sort of people who show respect to few and kindness to none, I would have failed as your parent.

Courtesy, which, by the way, walks hand in hand with respect and kindness, should always be in your pocket, ready to be whipped out at a moment's notice.

So, here are your rules for its application:

1. Be as courteous as you possibly can, at all times and in all places, even if – actually *especially if* – the people to whom you are talking are being particularly stupid and annoying.

2. If someone else addresses you in a way that is less than courteous, indulge them and assume that they have a) had a really bad day; b) had too much to drink; or c) not had the advantage of reading this.

3. Keep being courteous even if the other person is your mother, father, sister or brother.

Follow these rules and not only will you have a wonderful day, but you will not feel stressed or harassed by any of the bad behaviour I've outlined.

And if you pay particular attention to point 3, then I won't have to shout at anyone. And the world will be a place of miraculous beauty and grace.

All because of Courtesy. Imagine that!

Because in the sheer epic randomness of life, when you boil it down, all that really matters is the way in which we engage with one another.

THE 35TH OF 50 THINGS

FAMILY

'If you cannot get rid of the family skeleton,
you may as well make it dance.'
George Bernard Shaw

FAMILY

Archbishop Desmond Tutu said, 'You don't choose your family. They are God's gift to you, as you are to them.'

That is definitely true of our blood families. You get born into a family unit, which is comprised of you and your parents and your siblings, if you have any. I would never pick a fight with an archbishop, but I can imagine that some people might argue that their Family is not necessarily a blessing to them. I understand that but I don't necessarily agree with it because whatever else your Family teaches you, at some level they teach you something about love, even if the lesson can sometimes go a bit awry in the delivery.

There's a great sign on the wall in your Auntie Sarah's kitchen that reads, 'Remember: as far as anyone knows, we're a nice, normal family!'

The thing is, every Family has its issues, every Family has its secrets, every Family has its problems. Part of the blessing of Family is the way it drives you crazy and makes you marvel that, out of all the people on the planet, you ended up being related to *these* people.

But that's how life works. The person opposite you at any moment in time, whomever they may be, is your teacher. The lesson they are here to teach you is the thing you need to learn.

How annoying is that?!

Well, of course, it's very annoying.

But the great thing is that as you get older, the word Family adopts a much broader meaning. As you grow up, you and your brothers and sisters find your life partners, and those people become Family. And their families become part of your extended Family. It gets broader all on its own.

Seriously, think for a second, about all the amazing Family I gained the day I married your mother.

But likewise, as you get older, the word Family can embrace anyone you wish, not just those to whom you are bound by blood or marriage. The word can contract and expand as required to include anyone who is meaningful in your life, anyone who has stood beside you through life's storms, anyone who has cheered for your own success and happiness as though it were their own.

Which brings us to the Fitzsimons!

When I was about five, my parents separated and later divorced. A few years after that, my father met and then lived with Nuala Fitzsimons for several years before they eventually married. So Nuala was a significant presence in my life for most of my formative years and, somehow, in a magical and quite mysterious way that I don't really understand, her Family became my Family.

Now, you must remember, although both my parents came from large families themselves, neither of them was particularly close to their brothers and sisters, and though we were friendly with our cousins, we were not close either. I have approximately thirty first cousins; they are all perfectly lovely people but we are not close; I am only in touch with two of them and I only have a phone number for one. So you get the picture: my wider blood Family was not pining for me, nor I them.

But the Fitzsimons Family, already extended and crazy anyway, was dysfunctional enough to admit me sight unseen, no questions asked.

And the weird thing is that, even after my father and Nuala separated and then divorced, and even later when Nuala passed away, the Fitzsimons Family did not dump me, but instead gave me a home-from-home in Dublin, an extended Family with whom to share beach holidays when you were all small, and a loving place in which to share Family occasions such as Christmas.

So if you only remember one thing about Family, please let it be this: while I fervently hope that you will always be Family to one another, 'Family' can mean whatever you wish it to. No one needs to be excluded. There is room for everyone.

COMPASSION

'Our task must be to free ourselves . . . by widening our circle
of compassion to embrace all living creatures and the whole
of nature in its beauty.'
Albert Einstein

COMPASSION

I'm writing this one in the early days of a new year which are, as you know from all your chatter about resolutions, traditionally a time when people like to reflect on what has happened over the past year, what's coming up in the new year, and how they might handle it if they are lucky enough to get a choice. And some of us make resolutions to give up old things, like smoking or watching too much TV or drinking during the week. And some of us take up new things like exercise (Amelia) and playing bridge or joining a book club (Mum), or recommitting to practising the piano (Esme). And for reasons that are both mysterious and obvious, most of us have given up by the end of the first week of January.

But this one is about Compassion and the reason for that is that I think it's the one resolution we could all have that would make the world a better place, instantly.

His Holiness the Dalai Lama said, 'If you want others to be happy, practise compassion. If you want to be happy, practise compassion.'

Coining the same idea with a different sentiment, Adam Gnade said: 'Be good to people. Even the shitty ones. Let the assholes be assholes. You'll sleep better.'

Hopefully by now you are getting the idea that expressing Compassion is a good idea. But what is it, exactly?

Compassion, I think, is the application of love and kindness wherever it is needed, without reserve. It is extending ourselves to those to whom we owe no obligation; trying to tend to their suffering or misfortune as though it were our own. It's caring for those who have fallen. It's empathy for suffering of any kind. And it is vital to our humanity.

If you go to the thesaurus, there are dozens of synonyms for Compassion, and that in itself is interesting. Firstly, it tells us that Compassion is really vital. Secondly, and this is the really good news, there is clearly a lot of it about if it needs two dozen different names to get through the day!

Because here's the thing about Compassion: just as you can never have too much, nor can you ever give too much. In fact, the more you give, the more you will find you have to give. And the more you can bring yourself to give, the better the world will be.

And there, right there, you have a glorious, extraordinary synergy of ideas between Albert Einstein and the Dalai Lama – which is not something I thought I would ever witness – and it just shows you how amazing the universe is, that that kind of crazy collision of ideas is even possible.

Recently I heard that someone I used to work with had been tragically widowed after a fifty-year marriage. The thing is, this person and I had fallen out badly and had not spoken for over twenty years. Now, time is a great healer and the pain of the situation had resolved itself for me, but there was still a teeny niggle. (I judge these things on whether or not I would willingly answer the phone to the person I might have a niggle with. There was definitely a niggle.) Anyway, when I heard about his bereavement I wrote to him and expressed my very sincere condolences for his loss. It was the right thing to do. The stuff that passed between us back then is ancient history – and in the way of these things, not even very interesting history. The point is, I acted out of Compassion for his grief, and my sincerity must have been apparent because he responded. I'm not saying we're having lunch anytime soon, but the niggle is gone now. So there was a benefit to this.

You see, Compassion is not just for the rest of the world. It's also for you. Just as I want you to make a life's practice out of extending it to others – friends, family, loved ones and strangers alike – so I want you to make a habit of gifting it to yourselves as well.

So start right now and imagine how amazing your life, and the lives of those around you, might be if you were to practise Compassion at every opportunity. Think about how wonderful you could make the world around you. And whichever of its names you choose to use, I think you can see that nothing done in the spirit of Compassion could actually make the world a worse place, now could it?

So give it a go, yeah? Remember, it starts with you, and it includes your brother/sister. Even parents qualify. And after that, have fun, go wild and throw it everywhere you can. The results will astound you.

THE 37TH OF 50 THINGS

CAREER

'I've learned that making a "living" is not the same thing
as "making a life".'

Maya Angelou

CAREER

Believe it or not, I try not to start every chapter with a definition, but when I looked up the definition for Career, there were two entries that were massively helpful. First of all, I got:

1. noun: an occupation undertaken for a significant period of a person's life and with opportunities for progress.
2. verb: move swiftly and in an uncontrolled way.

And the thing is, although those two definitions are at first sight completely unrelated, I have to tell you that in terms of my own Career, well it has definitely been something that has moved swiftly and in an uncontrolled way. That is to say, whatever I achieved in terms of the first definition was done in terms of the second. As I said at the beginning, it has been like trying to crazy-pave the yellow-brick road in pitch-darkness.

I'm not saying that that is particularly a good thing or a bad thing, but, as you know, I set out wanting to be a horse vet. Where did it all go wrong? Let's just say that I was found to be academically insufficient for the task. So after some years trying a number of jobs, I somehow Forrest-Gumped my way into the film business and, I have to admit, it really hasn't been so bad. I've always joked that my success could be attributed to the fact that I was considered too stupid to be dangerous, and who knows? Maybe that's true. But I've worked on some amazing projects and had some incredible experiences and none of that could have happened if I had refused to go with the flow. Mind you, one could argue that 'the flow' did not give me much choice in the matter! In the name of work, I have been stuck in a laundry lift with Julia Roberts, walked along a red carpet next to Cate Blanchett. I've circumnavigated the globe on a private jet, watched Antonio Banderas dancing in his underwear and eaten sushi with Cameron Diaz. I've been to Australia for the day, and I was there at the Cannes Film Festival when Will Smith persuaded Angelina Jolie to ride on the back of a plastic shark.

So, you could say that, although I had a plan of what my Career should have looked like, maybe careering through it all wasn't such a bad way to go!

Similarly, if you have a clear vision of where you want to go in life, that's great. I hope it works out exactly as you wish, and that you will achieve your vocation. But I also urge you to embrace the unexpected, the curve balls that look like ruining everything you have worked so hard to create, for these will be the turning points that make the story into the adventure that you could never have imagined! I could never have planned any of the amazing things that happened to me – nor the countless others I cannot mention here for fear of legal action! – but they were hilarious sideshows from the main event of whatever we happened to be doing to launch whichever movie we were working on at the time. We did a great job and, boy, did we have fun doing it. I can't begin to tell you how grateful I am for the amazing Career I have had, and for all the adventures yet to come.

So where do you go with this? My advice is this: be open to everything. Sure, have a plan of sorts, but don't be afraid to make adjustments. Life has a wonderful knack of surprising you, often at the moments when you least expect.

The other thing to remember is this: a Career is great but, as the aphorism goes, no one ever died expressing regret that they didn't spend more time at the office. As C.S. Lewis said, 'The home is the ultimate career. All other careers exist for one purpose, and that is to support the ultimate career.' (Which really brings me back to my main point: which is that nothing I've ever done in my life, in my Career or elsewhere, is ever going to be as important as the fact that I'm your dad. Nothing. Simples.)

For all those of us born without a huge trust fund, that's undoubtedly true. We have to earn a living and somehow make a life at the same time. And in order to make a life, you have to try and find your purpose, the thing you are here to do that no one else can do as well as you can. Very often it will be the thing you really love to do more than anything else, and if you can find that and nurture it and work very hard at it, not only will your work be a pleasure and your Career a wonderful lifetime of exploration and enjoyment, but you will be rewarded in ways you can't possibly see right now.

So go, go and explore everything. Find the thing that makes your heart leap with excitement and has you jumping out of bed in the morning. Find the thing that gives you joy. And do that. With all your heart. Turn up on time every day and do your best. The results will amaze you.

LUCK

'Luck is not chance
It's toil
Fortune's expensive smile
Is earned'
Emily Dickinson

LUCK

Luck is defined as 'success or failure apparently brought by chance rather than through one's own actions'.

Hmm, we'll see about that.

After all, as the playwright Terence, or Virgil, is supposed to have said in the second century BC, '*Fortuna Audaces Iuvat*' or, as we like to say, 'Fortune favours the brave.'

First, though, it is obvious to say that everyone wants to experience only good Luck. We wish each other 'Good luck!' all the time. No one wants bad Luck and, furthermore, only the saddest of souls would wish bad Luck on anyone. However, while it's true that most of us seem to be lucky some of the time, so it's also true, sadly, that most people's lives involve a bit of bad Luck. Misfortune, some would call it.

So where do I stand on the issue of Luck?

Well, I'm all for it. I believe in it, I sincerely hope I have plenty of the good sort, I definitely don't want the bad sort but, if we're being honest with one another here, I also don't rely on it.

Which is to say, I don't trust Luck to do my work for me.

Back to Terence then. Or Virgil.

Thomas Jefferson, the third president of the United States, said, 'I'm a great believer in luck, and I find the harder I work the more I have of it.' The golfer Arnold Palmer is supposed to have said something very similar. Pick your icon; president or golfing champion, they both lived by the same maxim.

Certainly I would agree with them, that the harder you work, the better prepared you are, the harder you have striven to attain your goals, the more likely you are to succeed. And if Luck is to be the difference between achieving your goals and not achieving them, well, all that extra preparation is perhaps likely to make you the one who spots the cubic centimetre of opportunity, the lucky break, when it appears.

But the trouble with Luck is that it's so capricious, it's hard to know when we have earned it enough. Sometimes we don't get the Luck we feel we deserve. Sometimes we don't get the thing we want, the thing we have worked hard to achieve. Sometimes we get bad Luck. Or do we? I wonder if, really, it's all just a question of perspective?

His Holiness the Dalai Lama said, 'Remember that sometimes not getting what you want is a wonderful stroke of luck.'

This, I have to say, is a very good thing to remember, especially in the face of what might appear to be a disappointing result. (I refer you again to my failed attempt to be an equine vet. There are people in the film business still chuckling over that.)

The thing you have to bear in mind is that in our family, as far as the cosmic lottery is concerned, we have already hit the jackpot.

You don't think so?

Well, consider this: for a start we are all enjoying the rudest of health. If you don't think that is fortunate, try bad health and let me know how that works out for you.

Furthermore, we are lucky enough to live in a stable and secure democracy in an age of fairly enlightened tolerance.

And when you have finished enjoying the freedom of living in that fairly enlightened and tolerant democracy, the chances are that you're going to go to bed tonight on a full stomach, in a bed of your own, under a roof that is safe and secure. Should you need a glass of water in the night, there are gallons of it waiting to flow freshly from a tap, and, tomorrow, when you have enjoyed a proper breakfast and are about to curse the process of studying in which you are engaged, try to remember that you are part of a select group of people who have unfettered access to a world-class education.

You see where I'm going with this, right? We already have so much for which to be grateful. We are already so damn lucky.

So celebrate your innate good fortune every day, and then work hard, and see how much luckier you get.

COMPARISON

'Personality begins where comparison ends.'
Karl Lagerfeld

COMPARISON

Comparison is a tough one. It's something that is almost inevitable in daily life – people compare you to your siblings or your friends – and certainly in business, where no new venture gets going without a business plan based on historical comparisons, but honestly, it's a bugger of a thing. It can suck the oxygen out of a room quicker than a bullet through a fuselage.

In my humble opinion, Comparison, applied incorrectly, has the potential to cause more unnecessary misery than almost anything else. Whoever said comparisons are odious was right on the money.

Teddy Roosevelt, the eco-minded Nobel Prize-winning US president, said many clever things, including, 'Speak softly and carry a big stick,' which is also exceedingly good advice. But as far as Comparison is concerned, he nailed it: He said, 'Comparison is the thief of joy.'

Which is exactly what I am getting at.

I have seen people live disappointing lives because they could never stop comparing themselves and their achievements with those of others. But it's just so pointless. Everyone has a different path to tread, a different life to lead. It doesn't make their path better or worse than yours, just different.

Of course, sometimes it's impossible not to make comparisons, but while it's OK to visit occasionally, it's a dangerous place in which to live.

Think about it this way: to an outsider, the Duke and Duchess of Cambridge have an amazing life; they have several incredible homes and are cared for by a huge retinue of loyal servants; they get to visit the most amazing places in the world; everyone wants to meet them; and one day, as time marches on, they will be King and Queen. How amazingly cool and wonderful it must be to be them.

Really, though?

You can't begin to compare your life with theirs. They are heirs to the House of Windsor and one day will be our Heads of State. Other than Prince William's father and grandmother, no one else on the planet has an existence that can begin to truly compare with theirs. Their entire lives will be lived in service to this country; they can't vote, they are followed everywhere and they must live under a cast-iron self-discipline to avoid ever knowingly putting a foot wrong in public life. And whatever the media or politicians or anyone else ever says about them or their wider family, they can never respond.

My point is this: that's the life God gave them. There might be days in your life when you wish you had their life. Or if not them, the Beckhams. Or Mick Jagger. Get over it. God has a plan for you, a plan that is unique to you and fits your life perfectly. Make the best you can of that plan and don't waste energy or time making futile comparisons.

Now, I chose William and Kate to make the point, but in reality I'm also talking about your friends, your peer group and your siblings. Whatever Comparison you are tempted to make, drop it now, and leave it by the back door. It's not helping anyone, least of all you. Someone will always be richer, taller, prettier, smarter, cuter, funnier, faster, better connected, have more friends on Facebook or followers on Instagram. It doesn't matter. No one else can be you. Your innate worth – and you are priceless – cannot be calculated by the sum total of people who have 'liked' your posts on whatever social platform is in vogue this morning. You are beautiful and unique and no statistics can diminish that truth.

I learned the hard way not to compare when I started working in the film industry. You can't keep your head straight if you are constantly wondering why such-and-such a film star is in the position they are in and you are the human equivalent of whatever life form it is that treads water at a sewerage outlet. If I wasted time comparing my abs to Hugh Jackman's I would never get out of bed in the morning. No point. (I have to admit, I think that meditation helped, because it helped to shut off the noise, the shouting in my head about how inadequate I was. But in truth, I also realised how hard people in my industry work to stay fit, maintain their craft, maintain their appearance, etc., etc.)

The thing is, God never made two of anything the same, not even a snowflake. Nothing in creation has an exact duplicate. Every single thing in nature is unique. Your job is to be the best *you* that you can be. As the saying goes, you might as well because everyone else is taken.

So any kind of Comparison is irrelevant. Right?

Exactly! So do what Lagerfeld said: go with personality. Be unique!

THE 40TH OF 50 THINGS

MONEY

'The people who say that money can't buy happiness just don't know where to shop.'
Kathy Lette

MONEY

So, this is the last of the so-called 'Dinner Party Unmentionables' – we already did sex, religion and politics, remember?

Money, it is often said, is the root of all evil. That's actually a misquote. It should read, 'The love of money is the root of all kinds of evil.' Though Mark Twain coined it slightly differently when he said, 'The lack of money is the root of all evil.'

The thing about Money is that, like any form of energy, it's entirely neutral and it's entirely up to you how you use it. In the same way that electricity can be used just as efficiently to execute people as it can to keep babies in incubators alive, so Money can be used for good means or ill.

It's important that you get this straight, because too many people are going around with the idea that there isn't enough Money or that you have to be dishonest to be wealthy or that Money will corrupt you. That is all rubbish. All Money does is give you choices. Money allows you to do things that you would not be able to do otherwise. But it does not, cannot, make you evil. If you are already a bad person, Money will allow you to express it more easily, that's all. If you are the kind of person who thinks it is OK to take what is not yours because you want it, Money may inspire you to theft. But be clear: it's not the Money that's in the wrong in that situation.

The good news is that the opposite is also true. If you are a shining soul who wants to make the world a better and happier place, Money will help you to do that, too. But since the one thing that newspapers can't sell is good news, you're less likely to hear about philanthropy. Honestly, though, the amount of good that people are doing with their riches is extraordinary and is to be celebrated. Truly remarkable things are being achieved by generous people donating their Money to good works. Bill and Melinda Gates have donated their fortune to the Gates Foundation – giving huge sums of Money to finding cures for malaria, TB and HIV/AIDS. And they are not alone. Many, many wealthy people are changing lives for the better.

But back to us normal people for a second.

Oscar Wilde said, 'When I was young I thought that money was the most important thing in life. Now that I am old, I know that it is.'

You can always count on Oscar for a good quotation, but the thing is, he was right. To me, Money represents freedom, the freedom to make better choices. Not necessarily the freedom to always do what I want – though doing that or not doing that would also be a choice – but the freedom to make that choice, rather than to be in the position of having no choice to make. To me, that is real wealth, having a free choice rather than a forced one. And if it is Money which makes all the difference, so be it.

In the early stages of my career, a couple of people tried to suborn me. On the first occasion a TV producer of a well-known chat show suggested that if I could steer a certain film star on to their show I might enjoy a financial reward. And on another occasion a vendor who had a lucrative contract with the company that employed me proposed I take a luxury holiday at his expense to ensure that the contract was renewed. Now, here's the thing: if you're going to sell your soul to the devil, make sure to get a good price. I am relieved to be able to tell you, honestly, that in neither case was I tempted. It wasn't even a quandary. The price of that Money would have been unbearable.

Fortunately, the French philosopher Voltaire coined this epithet on the matter: 'Don't think money does everything or you are going to end up doing everything for money.' So that's that settled. It's good to have lines in the sand!

The point to remember is that Money is just a value system that mankind invented to make life more straightforward at the market. Think about it: we invented Money. It does not own us, so whether you let it rule or ruin you is up to you.

And while I know that many of the situations in which people suffer daily can be readily alleviated by Money, I urge you not to let your lives be ruled by it. It works for us, not the other way around.

THE 41ST OF 50 THINGS

FORGIVENESS

'*To err is human: to forgive, divine.*'
Alexander Pope

FORGIVENESS

When we came to live in this house, the hard stone floor in the kitchen was something of a revelation: in our previous house the lino had offered a softer landing whenever we dropped anything fragile. One day, Charlie, who was then aged four, dropped a cup on the floor, and as they cleared up the pieces, Mum explained to him that the new floor was not very forgiving and that he would need to take more care in future. A couple of days later, we overheard Charlie telling Amelia (who was two) that the new floor had no Forgiveness in it. It's a sweet example of childlike innocence, but he was spot on about the floor.

It's not always an easy thing to master, Forgiveness. It can stick in the throat a bit.

When I was younger, the thing I hated about Forgiveness was having to say 'I forgive you' when I really didn't feel it. It made me so angry to have to forgive anyone – my brother or sister, usually – when I knew that they were not sorry, anyway, and had only apologised because they had been told to, and I certainly did not feel inclined to let them off the hook either.

But I had a moment of awakening with Forgiveness when I was in my early twenties and it sort of helped me to reach an accommodation with it. Basically, I was the victim of a harmless practical joke. It was undoubtedly hilarious from one point of view, but from mine it was quite upsetting. The point was, I knew I had no choice other than to forgive it immediately, because otherwise it could have ruined a great friendship. And as I did, I realised that in some circumstances it was, indeed is, possible to consciously choose to forgive someone, rather than hang on to the pain of the situation. (Hmm, interesting. There's a choice available here.)

A few years later, as I took the first heady steps on the path to becoming the eccentric figure you know and love today, I read a self-help book by a writer called Louise Hay. On the subject of Forgiveness she said something like this: Forgiveness does not mean condoning another person's bad behaviour; rather, Forgiveness means releasing yourself from the self-righteous pain and indignation that goes with being the victim of someone else's actions. I may have paraphrased that but essentially what she was saying was that I didn't need to involve the other person in order for Forgiveness to take place.

So, not only could I choose, I could do it without an embarrassing or painful conversation. And I would be the one who benefited. I could move from the stone floor to the lino without an argument.

That was such a revelation. In that moment my whole understanding of Forgiveness changed. It no longer mattered if the other person was even sorry; Forgiveness meant that I was released from whatever the dynamic was that had caused the situation in the first place. Brilliant.

In a way I was lucky that the person who had upset me was such a great friend. It meant the stakes were really high. I had to decide quickly if I was going to let the upset be more important than their friendship. And you know me: I can sulk.

But there was no premium in delay, no worthwhile secondary gain in maintaining a position of lonely isolation on a barren high ground. The only thing to do was take a deep breath and let it go.

But again, go back to what Louise Hay said. She talked about the self-righteous indignation. It's a short way of saying that I could potentially have turned it into a starring role of victim in a play about wrongdoing. And I guess there's some mileage in that if you fancy playing that part, but it would have cost me my friendship.

So I think the crux of the matter is this: Forgiveness is about releasing yourself. If it's not, if you are struggling with that, then it's more likely to be based on some kind of internal struggle where it's more important for you to be right (and wronged) than to be healed. So the key, to me at least, seems to be not to worry about other people. If they have hurt you and are conscious enough to apologise, then sure, forgive them. It will release you both. And if they have hurt you but not apologised, forgive yourself.

Yes, that's right. Forgive yourself. Let yourself off the hook and go and devote your time and energy to feeling great about the rest of your day, instead of giving a millisecond of time or a scintilla of energy to the idea that someone, somewhere, somehow hurt your feelings or violated you. Let yourself off the hook, let them worry about their own baggage and release yourself. Ultimately whatever they did, whatever they said, it will have taught you something, it will have made you wiser, possibly stronger, and possibly more compassionate.

Trust me on this: over time I have come to see that the people who hurt me, the people I have it in my power to forgive (or not), have taught me so much about life. I only wish I had thought to thank them properly at the time.

And you were right about the floor, Charlie!

THE 42ND OF 50 THINGS

JOY

'Joy is to fun what the deep sea is to a puddle. It's a feeling inside that can hardly be contained.'

Terry Pratchett

JOY

Joy doesn't get a lot of airtime these days. Everyone talks about happiness instead. Happiness is OK, but if you ask me, it's joy-lite.

You know the feeling? Joy is happiness distilled down into its most concentrated form; so powerful that it bursts out of you like sunbeams through a blind. If happiness was a cheese string, Joy would be mature vintage cheddar. It is clearly a state to be sought after and relished.

Actually, though, I don't believe that we need to seek it out at all because, in truth, it is our natural state of being. Good news, huh? Joyfulness is our default state, and babies and small children express it unconsciously at all times. I remember one summer afternoon when Esme was a toddler, watching her play in the spray from the garden sprinkler. Everyone was busy elsewhere, but she was dancing in and out of the watery rays, trying to catch the rainbow they were making, and brimming over with sheer Joy, laughter bubbling out of her in gurgles and even screams that were infectious to listen to. I am smiling now, remembering that unconfined Joy. I remember it as well when I look at the trampoline in the garden and think of you three playing on it every day that you possibly could, screaming with laughter.

As we get older, though, Joy just tends to get a bit covered up by everyday things like school and work, and the fatigue of commuting and paying the bills, as well as all the other emotional drama that goes on in the daily round of life.

But have no doubt, our Joy is always there, bubbling away under the surface, waiting for its chance to burst out in a laugh with a friend, or simply a feeling of exuberant well-being.

If we're lucky, at some point we wake up to the fact that somehow we have let our Joy get covered over, we learn to recognise that there are activities like sports and singing and, yes, even Scottish dancing (all forms of creative self-expression, please note!), which leave us feeling joyful because, in our attention to them, we forget the irritations of the daily grind and revert to our natural state. And in those heady moments we become our true, joyful selves again, little motes of dust dancing in the sun's rays.

But like all good things, there are terms and conditions; or to put it another way, there's a catch.

Joy has a twin. Sorrow. Where one goes, eventually the other must follow. I don't want to be a downer on Joy here, but if you think that life is never going to throw you anything except rose petals and hummingbirds, it's time to guess again.

In his spiritual classic *The Prophet*, Kahlil Gibran wrote:

> Some of you say, 'Joy is greater than sorrow,' and
> others say, 'Nay, sorrow is the greater.' But I say
> unto you, they are inseparable. Together they come,
> and when one sits alone with you at your board,
> remember that the other is asleep upon your bed.

Now, if you ask me, would I give away my Joy in order to escape sorrow? Well, of course I wouldn't. Just as Joy can be transformative because of its sheer beauty, so too can sorrow, which is just as beautiful in its own ways, and just as transformative.

Imagine how much the poorer our lives would be if we could never experience sorrow. How can you appreciate the light if you have never seen the shade? Rather than being diminished by your sorrow, your Joy is all the more precious because of the contrast.

The Indian poet Rumi had this to say:

> Sorrow prepares you for joy. It violently sweeps everything out of your house, so that new joy can find space to enter. It shakes the yellow leaves from the bough of your heart, so that fresh, green leaves can grow in their place. It pulls up the rotten roots, so that new roots hidden beneath have room to grow. Whatever sorrow shakes from your heart, far better things will take their place.

So what am I saying here? I'm saying that when sorrow finds you, embrace it, because if you embrace it, it will lead you to your Joy. Equally strongly, embrace your life, and every activity you undertake, because in aligning yourself with life you will experience the Joy of being present in the moment of *now*, rather than in the frustrating agony of contemplating the past or anticipating the future.

And in finding your Joy, remember that you always have it and that it is the way you are meant to live. Too many good people have forgotten that they are entitled to be joyful.

Pierre Teilhard de Chardin: 'Joy is the infallible sign of the presence of God.'

To which I would only add this: life can be drudge and gloom or it can be a party. And if you turn up like a good guest, let your Joy flow freely and celebrate every moment, you may just find it's been thrown in your honour.

THE 43RD OF 50 THINGS

HUMILITY

'There is nothing noble in being superior to your fellow man;
true nobility is being superior to your former self.'
Ernest Hemingway

HUMILITY

Well, we're whipping through them now, and, with the end in sight, I was starting to feel a bit complacent. Then I noticed that the next topic on my list was Humility, which pulled me up slightly. So now, smugness cast firmly aside, here it is.

Humility is defined as 'the quality of having a modest or low view of one's importance' and its synonyms are: modesty, humbleness, meekness, lack of pride, lack of vanity, diffidence, unassertiveness.

Let's be honest, it doesn't sound very sexy, does it?

But actually, Humility – though by definition it could never celebrate itself – is probably a quality that you should celebrate, and even cultivate. Because Humility, applied correctly, is the dignified and discreet pinprick to the over-inflating ego. It's the gentle reminder that, apart from anything else, no matter where you go in the world, no matter what wealth you accumulate, no matter what honours are bestowed upon you, it is undoubtedly true, as renowned French author and inventor of the modern essay Michel de Montaigne wrote, that 'On the highest throne in the world, we still sit only on our own bottom.'

And why is it so important that we all go out of our way to remember something so obvious?

While I know that, to the untrained eye, Humility might

appear really a little unexciting, it's actually a diamond in the rough. Humility is the thing that will make it possible to look at yourself in the mirror every morning; it is the thing that will stop you ever getting so far above yourself or those around you that you can no longer relate to them, no longer understand their problems or the issues they are facing. Humility will keep you kind, it will keep you honest, and every time you invoke it, it will inspire your compassion. Humility is the virtue of the truly laid-back, those who can tolerate poor service in a restaurant and remain chilled and say, 'They're doing their best.'

That, I think, is what lies at the very heart of Humility: the recognition that everyone, everywhere, is doing their best, according to what they know, according to the level of consciousness under which they're operating. The rule of thumb is this: if they knew better, they'd do better. And ultimately the truth is that, whether or not it is comfortable for you to admit it to yourself, the same is true of you. So you have to forgive their shortcomings.

I seem to have gone around the houses on that a bit.

Lao Tzu, the Chinese philosopher after whom Taoism is named said:

> I have three precious things which I hold fast and prize. The first is gentleness; the second is frugality; the third is humility, which keeps me from putting myself before others. Be gentle and you can be bold; be frugal and you can be liberal; avoid putting yourself before others and you can become a leader among men.

And that's Humility, I think. It's your safety harness against colossal and self-consuming arrogance. It's your shield against over-vaunting pride.

Even when he was president of South Africa, Nelson Mandela insisted on making his own bed every day. Instead of allowing his elevation to the headship of state to inflate his ego, he chose the opposite, remaining as humble as when he was a prisoner on Robben Island. And by never placing himself or his needs above anyone else's, he commanded the love of a people and united a nation.

THE 44TH OF 50 THINGS

WORK

'I like work: it fascinates me. I can sit and look at it for hours.'
Jerome K. Jerome

WORK

Never forget: Work is a four-letter word.

Work is a bit like money, inasmuch as there are strongly held and hugely divergent philosophies on the matter. For example, a lot of people think that if you don't Work hard, i.e. if you are not suffering miserably and it doesn't feel like real pain, then it doesn't really count as Work.

But Confucius said, 'Choose a job you love, and you will never have to work a day in your life.'

Of course, the truth is that it's not that simple. Do the majority of people really have that much of a choice?

I would definitely say that suffering through Work is not mandatory. In fact, I would say that even if you are doing Work that is not vocational, even if it's Work you are doing just for the wages, do it as cheerfully and as well as you possibly can. Firstly, the time will pass faster; secondly, the people around you will appreciate and respond to your cheerfulness; and thirdly, you may find that, actually, you can enjoy it; for Work, like virtue, can be its own reward. Too often, though, we decide in advance that a job is going to be a miserable experience and hey – guess what? – it becomes one!

The thing is, you are all coming to that time in your lives when you are probably going to have to do some so-called grunt work, that perhaps you would not have chosen, in order to get yourselves to a place where you can do the Work you would love to do. But if you decide to love all of it, no matter what it is, amazing things can happen. Just changing your approach, your attitude, your energy, can transform the situation, and with it your experience.

When I was about nineteen, I got a job at the local racecourse, working with the ground staff. One of my first tasks was to mow the grass around the jump fences on the course. Now it was high summer and at that time I suffered very badly with hay fever, and by the time I had mown the grass around the first fence, my eyes and nose were streaming and I was wheezing like a punctured bellows. When the foreman came to inspect my Work he was amazed that I hadn't just refused to mow the grass, or stopped when my eyes started to water, but he was also impressed by my determination and willingness to do whatever it took to get the job done. The rest of the week I was excused mowing, and the crew teased me a bit, but I was welcome back at any time.

Now, if you have been paying attention for the past few years, you will have heard me say more than once, 'Turn up on time, do your best.' Trust me on this, wherever you are, it's great advice, but when it comes to Work, it's invaluable. The thing is, a lot of people simply don't do it. They resent having to Work, resent being told what to do by someone they regard as unfit to be their boss. And it shows. (Of course, you have to be compassionate about this stuff. You never know what other people have to endure elsewhere in their lives.)

But how do you know what your dream job is? I mean, I know we'd all love to be Taylor Swift or Miranda Hart, but those jobs are already taken so what's your gig going to be?

Rumi said, 'Everyone has been made for some particular work, and the desire for that work has been put in every heart.'

So I guess that means if you sit still and listen to yourself, somehow, sometime, you will get a hint about what it is you are meant to do with your life. Sometimes, we don't hear the message properly, and I would strongly urge you not to be discouraged. It may take more than one attempt to get it right. (Horse vet, remember.) But the good news is that you will learn as much from the near misses and the outright disasters as you will from the staggering successes. In fact, I think the mistakes are crucial if you are ever going to make a success of your Work, so celebrate the disasters. They will teach you valuable lessons.

In many ways, school is a great training ground for Work. It's where you get to develop your interpersonal skills; hone your communication so that you don't create a trail of misunderstanding wherever you go; and it's where you get to work out, mostly through trial and error, whether you want to lark around at the back with your friends or if you want to give it your best shot and see how far you can go.

And that's not to say that every moment of school should be Work, but if you go with Confucius's thoughts on the matter, you can see how it can all become fun.

Do the thing you love the most and it will never feel like Work.

RELATIONSHIPS

'It only takes one to tango, as long as it's you.'
Chuck Spezzano

RELATIONSHIPS

In *Shirley Valentine*, the wonderful comedy by Willy Russell, there's a scene in which the eponymous heroine says, 'Marriage is like the Middle East: there's no solution.'

I've seen *Shirley Valentine* on stage and in the cinema, and that line gets a big laugh every time. Mostly from married people, men and women alike.

But the reason that line is so funny is that, while it's fundamentally true, it's also absurd.

And the same is true of all Relationships.

Of course, you can get away with that kind of comedic quip in films and plays, but in real life, you have to be more careful. The gender stereotyping or casual sexism which says that all men are unfeeling brutes who can't cook or do laundry is as accurate as the kind of recidivist thinking which says women can't reverse or read maps. In other words, at a personal level, it's bollocks because it fails to recognise nuance or complexity.

And the thing about Relationships is that they are as complex as the people involved.

I learned a long time ago that you should never attempt to draw conclusions about other people's Relationships. Firstly, it's absolutely none of your business, and secondly, you can't possibly know what's really going on. All you can ever know is what either of the people in the relationship has told you, and though they might be willing to put their hands on a Bible and swear they are telling the truth, it's *their* truth they are telling, and as we all know, that can be subjective, especially in a relationship. Similarly, if you are one of the people in the relationship, you can only ever be completely sure about your side of it, and in my experience even then there can be doubt.

Growing up, I watched my mother and father in their various marriages – sometimes shaking my head in amazement at their stupidity (because, after all, I was a teenager and I knew everything) – and realised that often the reality of their life together was very different from the social front they presented to the wider world. But while on one level I saw people who appeared to be in denial about the fact that they were living in a war zone, I also saw people who loved each other, trying to do their best every day to overcome their own inner demons.

So here's the thing: I think your Relationships are a reflection of who you are, and I learned that from being in my own relationship with your mother. Sometimes I don't know what's going on and I'm an equal partner! But I know that the level to which I give to the relationship, I am rewarded in what I get back.

What does all this tell you about Relationships? Well, it tells you that they are fragile, they need lots of oxygen to survive, and without it they founder and fail very quickly. They can be volatile and passionate and steady and relaxing. They can drive you to the heights of joy and the brink of despair in a single evening. They can burn brightly for an hour or an eternity. And the quickest way to lose one is to take it for granted.

But what is oxygen for a relationship? I used to think it was love, but now I am not so sure. Love is such a variable emotion – when you start a relationship the passion is so overwhelmingly intense, if you tried to keep it up for more than six months I expect you'd die of exhaustion! A relationship that lasts is one in which the love remains, but it's a slightly less frantic passion that guides it. It's steadier but no less deep, just more manageable long term. I suspect that is the love on which most sustaining Relationships are based. But anyway, I don't think love is the oxygen of Relationships. I think the oxygen of Relationships is truth.

For just as people change over time, from day to day, so too do their Relationships. One of the most vital things in maintaining a relationship is to remain in touch with those changes. That requires one to be honest not only with one's partner, but also with oneself.

When your mum and I were engaged to be married, we were given an audio talk by an Indian spiritual guru who spoke about Relationships, and specifically marriage. He said a couple of things that have always stayed with me. One of them was about the importance of talking. He said, you must talk. And when you have finished talking, you must talk some more. And then you must talk. Talk, talk, talk, talk, talk, talk, talk. And that, I guess, would be a very good way to stay current with the other person, to remain up to date with them and their feelings, as well as one's own.

The other thing that he said was amazing, and I have tried to do it, though I have not always succeeded. He said, for your marriage (relationship) to succeed, you must expect nothing from the other person and everything from yourself. But you both have to do it.

If you think about it, he was right. If only one of you ever did that, your relationship would not last long. It needs both of you to believe in the relationship and to support it. The thing is, sometimes, for various reasons, it may not be possible for both of you to do it at the same time. And that, I think, is what Chuck Spezzano was talking about. Sometimes, 'it only takes one to tango, as long as it's you'. If you take responsibility for your part of the relationship, the chances are that it will sustain.

Now, if they are so fragile and such hard work, why do we bother with them, these chimera-like Relationships? Well, because they define us, they make our existence on this planet more meaningful, they teach us about wonder and joy, about real love, about despair and hope and tolerance and compassion, and all of the virtues I have written about here, and many more besides. They teach us about the nature of sacrifice, and, truly, they give our lives meaning. I would not, could not, possibly be the man I am today if I had not met, fallen in love with and married your mother. I could not be your father. She has made me who I am and loved me into the bargain.

And so my advice to you, concerning Relationships, is this: whether they are starting or sustaining, evolving or ending, always treat the other person as you yourself would wish to be treated. Afford them every honour, respect and courtesy, as well as the love that they have earned from you.

For, as it goes in *Les Miserables*, 'To love another person is to see the face of God.'

Amen to that.

WISDOM

'Never let your sense of morals prevent you
from doing what is right.'
Isaac Asimov, *Foundation*

WISDOM

Confucius said, 'By three methods we may learn wisdom: first, by reflection, which is noblest; second, by imitation, which is easiest; and third by experience, which is the bitterest.'

And while experience may be the bitterest way to acquire Wisdom, it certainly seems to be the one most of us choose. But just as our life experiences are unique and subjective, so Wisdom can appear to vary enormously from person to person. Just as one man's meat is another man's poison, so one man's Wisdom . . . well, you get the idea. People will have very strongly held convictions about what is wise, what Wisdom actually is, and sometimes I think it gets mixed up with social mores.

But just as real morality rises above fashion or trend, so real Wisdom has the power to transcend workaday thinking. You will always know real Wisdom when you hear it because of the startling simplicity of its sound. In essence, Wisdom is truth, and when you hear it, it's so plain, so uncontrived, that you just recognise it immediately.

The thing is, it's not always popular.

So where am I going with this? Well, Wisdom is a hard nut to crack. First of all, it takes years to acquire it, and then, when you finally get some, you have to tone it down a bit. (No one likes a smart-arse.)

For me, if I have garnered any pearl of Wisdom in my time on this planet, it's this: I really don't know anything.

And where has that got me? Well, I'm ready to be wrong about absolutely everything; and I've learned that sometimes you choose the path, and sometimes the path chooses you; and I've learned that you may as well go with the flow because, if you don't, the current will take you anyway; and, finally, I'm no longer convinced that the universe operates only for me to be happy.

And in all of that Wisdom, if indeed that is what it is, there is a huge sense of relief.

Relief, I guess, at letting go of all that stuff that used to claim me. Relief at not having to hold firm opinions about absolutely bloody everything.

Such as? Well, anything I needed to be right about, for a start. As pretty much anyone who knows me will attest, I'm not afraid to make a fool of myself any day of the week. Why? Because I learned a long time ago that most people are not actually paying that much attention or haven't noticed or simply don't care. And me? I stopped caring around the same time I realised that worrying what other people thought was as effective as King Canute commanding the tide to turn back. So why should I be afraid of being thought a fool by people whose minds are probably made up before I opened my mouth anyway?

Several people, including Maurice Switzer and Abraham Lincoln, are quoted as having said, 'It is better to remain silent at the risk of being thought a fool, than to talk and remove all doubt of it.'

While I think that remark is very witty, I no longer hold it to be true. I now think that it is better to speak up and tell your truth pleasantly rather than to remain silent and allow ignorance to prevail.

Finally, although Wisdom is gained from the experience of years past, the thing to remember is that it is only of value if we allow it to guide our path forwards.

My wish for you, with regards to Wisdom, comes from Jonathan Swift: 'May you live every day of your life.'

For in that way you will gain experience, and that will bring you Wisdom, and in your Wisdom you will recognise the beauty of life and the great gift you have been given. And when you recognise all those blessings, you will be happy.

THE 47TH OF 50 THINGS

POLITICS

'A week is a long time in politics.'
Harold Wilson

POLITICS

I thought this chapter on Politics was all settled. I felt I had written about Politics very eloquently and worked out that for me, writing as a layman, it is essential to maintain a healthy balance between cynicism and hope; that I should try to maintain a healthy distance while yet remaining fully aware of what is going on; and to try never to assume that politicians are always acting out of self-interest rather than a desire to serve the country.

That was all fine right up until the summer of 2016, which turned upside down the entire UK and European political establishment in a way that I have never seen before.

The UK voted for Brexit.

Now, while I'm aware of the aphorism that says that nothing dates faster than being current, I don't feel I can leave you with generic platitudes about Politics and ignore a period that contained the most exciting political episode of my entire life.

So here we go.

On 23 June 2016, the long-awaited referendum on the UK's continuing membership of the EU was held. I never stay up for election results, and as I went to bed that night, pundits and polls alike were confidently predicting a majority for 'Remain' in what had been a hard-fought campaign that had been much criticised for focusing only on negativity. As I turned out the light, Twitter was buzzing with rumours that the leader of UKIP, Nigel Farage, was about to concede defeat. Yet, when I awoke six hours later, it was to the news that that confident prediction had been turned on its head; the 'Leave' campaign had won and the UK's forty-year membership of the EU was to end.

Now, whether you wanted to Remain or Leave, whether you believe that we're going to sink faster than a brick or we're going to be fine (and, by the way, we're going to be fine), one thing is clear: what followed was a month of political blood-letting which made the news much more exciting than usual. Real-time events were moving so quickly that the news bulletins were struggling to keep up. Politicians were pulling cards out of their sleeves faster than magicians can pull rabbits out of top hats.

The morning after the Brexit result, UK Prime Minister David Cameron, having led the Remain campaign, resigned. The country was in shock, but Cameron was clear: having campaigned for Remain and believing that the UK was better in Europe, he was no longer the right man for a job which now entailed negotiating the terms of our exit from Europe.

But no sooner than that announcement had hit the airwaves, and not to be outdone, Nigel Farage also resigned, having, he said, 'achieved his objectives'. While the commentators began to digest the idea that the people who had delivered the referendum and its result were now absenting the scene, what we all failed to realise was that the fun was only just beginning.

Michael Gove MP, who had been a leader of the Leave campaign, pulled an act of betrayal that was Shakespearean in its scale and impact, when he withdrew his support for his political partner Boris Johnson and put himself forward for the

Tory leadership contest, leaving the former London Mayor no choice but to stand down. (Gove then failed to achieve a ranking in the ballot of Tory MPs and himself had to drop out, so 'yah boo sucks' to him, but still the fun continued.)

The run-off for the Tory leadership then came down to a contest between two women: Andrea Leadsom and the former Home Secretary, Theresa May. When Leadsom stood down, Theresa May accepted the leadership, becoming only the second woman prime minister in British history.

Now, by anyone's measure, all of that is enough political excitement for a year, let alone three weeks, but still there was more. The Labour party, feeling a little out of it, no doubt, decided to try to oust their own leader, Jeremy Corbyn, because, they said, he had not been vocal enough in his support for the Remain campaign. (One suspects that they were also concerned about his electability at a time when a general election looked very possible.)

And, of course, on top of that, there were wider ramifications: discussion about the Scottish referendum on secession from the UK was revived; the border between Northern Ireland and the Republic became a live issue again; and everyone in Europe seemed to be very cross with us. France's Axelle Lemaire, the deputy minister of digital affairs, very appositely tweeted, 'Brexit politics in the UK is like *Game of Thrones* meeting *Monty Python.*'

But just when you thought it was safe to turn on the news again, the Chilcot Report, the government's own investigation into the 2003 invasion of Iraq and the deposition of Saddam Hussain, was finally published, just two weeks after Brexit, once again filling our newspapers and TV screens with images of a bullying tyrant and his cronies recklessly pursuing their own agenda regardless of the cost to human life. But whatever your thoughts about George W. Bush and Tony Blair, the long-awaited report marked another extraordinary episode in the political life of our nation. I'm inclined to think that the ongoing political hubbub around the publication of Chilcot meant that a lot of people got away with murder – maybe metaphorically, maybe not – but I'm also reassured that the report pretty much confirmed that which we already suspected: the decision to go to war was taken long before it was ever debated in Parliament or discussed in Cabinet; that the intelligence put in front of MPs was faulty; that good soldiers died needlessly because they were not properly equipped; and that no one had a clue what we would do once the objective had been achieved. It's not comforting, but at least we know that we were not wrong in our assumptions.

All of which – Brexit, Cameron, Farage, Gove, Johnson, Leadsom, May, Corbyn, Chilcot, Bush, Blair – leads me to conclude one thing: just as Politics is about the governance of everyday life, so politicians are humans, like you and me. And as history is created by series of human actions, made in single moments by ordinary people doing extraordinary things, so the same can be said for Politics. What modern media has done is to shine a light on everything that happens and allow it to be reported so swiftly that the acts speak for themselves without a hastily applied veneer of PR. In this month of political disruption, things literally moved too fast for the spin doctors to control them.

And if there is one thing to take home from all of this excitement, it's this: not engaging in the political life of our nation is as big a decision as engaging. And since it's clear that the people doing it are as likely to err as you are, you should not believe that it's an elitist activity in which you can have no say. If nothing else, the referendum on Brexit reminds us of the importance of a single vote, a single voice; while the Chilcot inquiry, finally published after years of clamour for the truth, proves that by working together, people can define their own Politics and create their own history.

I'll vote for that.

PARENTHOOD

'You know your children are growing up when they stop
asking you where they came from and refuse to tell
you where they're going.'
P.J. O'Rourke

PARENTHOOD

There is a thing floating around on Facebook that says: 'If you want to know what it's like to be a parent: take all your belongings; throw them on the floor; pick them up again; repeat for infinity.'

And in truth, it is a bit like that. It's messy, and unending, but as well as involving a lot of tidying up, Parenthood is the most amazing miracle going.

For starters, one of the most amazing things about Parenthood is that it is by far the most significant thing that most of us who are lucky enough to be parents will ever do in our lives. (I say 'most of us' because some people achieve remarkable things that surpass even the miracle of Parenthood and change everyone's lives. For example, Sir Tim Berners-Lee invented the internet. I'm proud of being your father, but I think the internet kind of trumps that in terms of impact on the wider world. Although who knows what you kids may achieve?) Anyway, you get my point, which is that Parenthood is the biggest thing most of us ever do.

Yet here's another amazing thing: the beautiful paradox of Parenthood is that, in my view, the moment in which we conceived you is a secret known only to God. At best we can only guess, but never with any real accuracy, the moment we used our bodies to create another life. It is truly a miracle.

When Charlie was a couple of weeks old I remember a friend who had been holding him, handing him back to me and saying, 'Now you know how much your mum and dad loved you.' And, of course, among the many other amazing lessons Parenthood teaches you, that is one of the first because truly – and I can tell you this from experience – anyone who stayed up with you night after night, cradling you in their tired arms and singing softly to you as you cried, in spite of the fact that they were so exhausted from sleep deprivation that they went to sleep under their desk at work the next day (yes, really): those people love you unconditionally.

Likewise, anyone who soothed you at two o'clock in the morning as your first teeth painfully pushed their way into your mouth, when all they could do was rub your gums and deny themselves yet more sleep; those people loved you. As did anyone who gently wiped you clean as they changed your filthy nappy for the thousandth time, and all of this without a word of thanks (because you couldn't talk) or even a smile? Trust me, those people love you.

Which is just as well because that is only the start of Parenthood. Once the little bastards start walking and talking, that's when the trouble begins!

To be a parent is to have parts of your soul walking around outside your body. You are a hostage to fortune. It is tiring and expensive and sometimes thankless, not to mention grindingly exhausting and often a bit scary. Plus there is the indignity of being covered in vomit, snot and saliva on a daily basis. But not one bit of that matters. It is a price we willingly pay for the privilege of loving you; of loving you and being your parent.

The writer Peter De Vries said, 'The value of marriage is not that adults produce children, but that children produce adults.'

This is absolutely true. We do things for our children that we would never do for ourselves, or even our other loved ones. Children define you. When you become a parent you have to work out where you stand, what your values are, because you are about to bring a life into the world and shape it for the first eighteen or so years of its existence. Everything you do will be influential to a level you have never achieved before. Another miracle, and also a warning.

And all too soon, just as the teething and potty-training and sleepless nights come to an end, so the letting go begins.

But where does it begin, this letting go? Looking back, I think it probably begins on the first day of school. My father, your Irish grandpa, once said to me, 'You never realise, until it's too late, that from the day your children are born you are preparing them to leave you.' When you were little, I could pretend I didn't hear him correctly, but now, as you are all teenagers, I have to face that stark reality, that our job – the first phase of it anyway – is coming to an end.

But, oh my darlings, how we shall miss you. Every meal, every question, every journey to school, every Christmas, every birthday, every holiday, every precious moment is a special treasure for which I cannot thank you enough. For, as Peter De Vries says, you have made me who I am.

My beautiful boy, Charlie, you embody wit and charm and you drive me crazy, not least because when you apply yourself to something you make it look so easy.

And my darling Amelia, so beautiful, so strong, so vulnerable, so funny; I am already praying for your future husband!

And Esme, my little star, the brilliant listener, who uses my own logic to defeat me in arguments, and who has the kindest of hearts.

You are all exceptional people and I am so proud to be your loving dad.

If I am in any way a good or decent person, it is because I had the immense and overwhelming privilege to be your father.

THE 49TH OF 50 THINGS

HOME

'Home is where the heart is.'
Pliny the Elder

HOME

The dictionary defines Home, rather tediously, as 'the place one lives permanently'. Snore.

On the other hand, Pliny the Elder's quote about Home is universally recognised, even if we didn't know it was attributed to that great man: 'Home is where the heart is.'

And that is much more helpful, for it not only conjures up feelings, but also images, of happy times in a place of comfort and safety; of a place to which we can retreat, to escape from the outside world.

Home.

Go on, say it! Even saying it out loud is comforting. As Jane Austen once wrote in *Emma*, 'There is nothing like staying at home for real comfort.'

But it's more fundamental, more important, than comfort (I can't say that word without thinking of cushions), even more important than that, isn't it? It's such a primordial need.

Because, I suppose, even if you happen not to live in a palace or a castle, as most of us don't, the point is that Home is the place where we can pull up the drawbridge and feel really safe. (That's if we are lucky, of course – countless people and their children do not feel safe in their own homes, we should remember that.)

There is a bit of old wives' flimflam which says, 'You have to give your children roots so that they can grow wings.' Personally, I think the old wives had been hitting the cider a bit when they came up with that one. Not exactly pithy, is it? But while I find the expression a tad clumsy, if you give it a moment to sink in, the sentiment is spot on.

When I was growing up, I noticed my friends, who had what I regarded as more stable and possibly more nurturing backgrounds than I, had no problem whatsoever going away from Home. In fact, they were so confident of its permanence, so comfortable in their place there, knowing that it would be waiting for them whenever they returned, that they could leave at will with nary a backward glance and give it scant thought while they were away. Being homesick was not their norm.

Weirdly, in my situation, I found that ease of departing a very hard state to acquire. Looking back, I think it was because I did not share their confidence in my Home; neither in its permanence, nor even in my own welcome there; so, paradoxically, I found it hard to leave and constantly needed to return. I still don't really know why, and that's just one of the little wrinkles that makes my life the beautiful mystery it is today! Maybe I was afraid they might have moved and not told me? Whatever. As my Grandma Elsie used to say, it will all be the same in a hundred years.

But I think what my friends knew innately, for I don't think it was ever said out loud, was what Maya Angelou wrote about when she said, 'You can never go Home again, but the truth is you can never leave Home, so it's all right.'

They knew without being told that it was all right.

As an adult, leaving my slightly dysfunctional Home and going out into the world, I knew what I wanted my own family's Home to be, I just had to work with other people's models rather than my own.

And you know what? It worked out brilliantly. Your mother and I both like space. So we found a place with space. With big, airy rooms for our growing family, and plenty of open ground for running about, and beautiful trees for climbing and shade. Space to breathe, space to grow, space to live. We have tried to make it a place of comfort, a place of safety and, most important of all, a place of happy memories. I guess history will be the judge of whether we succeeded, but one day when you were all little, Amelia was telling me about something exciting that had happened, and when I asked where it had happened, she said, 'On the dancing side of the kitchen.' So I think we may have got it right; we may just have created the place we intended to create: a place of fun, a place of love; your Home.

George Washington once said, 'I had rather be on my farm than be emperor of the world.' I know exactly what he meant. Whenever I have been travelling, no matter how exotic, how amazing the trip has been, when I get out of the car on our drive I stand and look up at the sky and draw deep breaths, taking in not only the air, but also the place. I guess I am restoring myself, I am letting myself know that I am really Home.

But what of all this? Well, I guess it's this: I don't think it matters where you go, or for how long, because this place, this Home, will always be with you. It will always be here and even when it's not here, you will always have it in your hearts.

And when you come to settle down to make homes of your own, for your own families, I hope that your Home has given you enough so that you can hold a vision of what kind of Home you want to create, the kind of place you wish it to be.

If you're not sure, start with your heart. That's where you will find it.

THE 50TH OF 50 THINGS

LOVE

'Love is the answer.'
John Lennon

LOVE

Well, my darlings, here we are, finally, at the fiftieth of *The 50 Things*. I have loved writing it. It's made me think about aspects of my own life in more detail than I have been able to convey here; it's made me question my motives in some of my past actions; and it's made me aware that we, by which of course I really mean 'I', must always fight to overcome our cynicism. I must remain full of wonder, like a small child. It is the correct way to view the world.

I don't know if I got the order right, but somehow it does seem fitting to have left Love until the end, though by now I think it's pretty clear that ultimately, whatever heading you put at the top of the page, all of these chapters have really been about Love.

And actually, what has been 50 Things really could have just been one thing, because, as I say, in the end it all boils down to Love, which is no surprise really because, as I have been telling you all these years, John Lennon was right: Love really is the answer. You don't even have to trust me on that one; in time you will come to know the truth of it.

On the day that each of you was born, I held you in my arms as your marvellous, astonishing, exhausted mother looked on (you all weighed over nine pounds; no wonder she was exhausted), and as I marvelled at your sheer perfection, at the staggering miracle of your life officially beginning, I made a silent but unbreakable vow to you that I would always look after you; that, no matter what happened, I would always be there to take care of you. And every parent who ever reads this is nodding right now because they did exactly the same thing, as will you when your turn comes to be a parent and witness the sheer overwhelming magnificence of that miracle of Love. (But by the way, this Love is not just a parent–child thing; I use that because it's the most profound example I have ever experienced, but Love is Love whichever way it flows.)

Anyway, where was I? Right, I was talking about making an unbreakable vow . . . So, as you know, when this started I was thinking about the fact that I'm now over fifty, that whichever way you cut it I'm likely over halfway through, and I wanted to leave you guys something that would live on. Partly I was inspired by the death of my own mother at far too young an age, realising that there are conversations which I can never now have with her. (Or at least, I can, but they tend to be a bit one-sided and frustrating.)

Similarly, as my father retreats ever further behind the veil of Alzheimer's, there are fewer conversations of meaning to be had with him, fewer questions that can be asked, or answered.

What I'm saying is that I realised nothing should be taken for granted.

And I remembered when I first heard Jeffrey Katzenberg talking about when he took over the animation department at Disney. First of all, he looked around in dismay at the chaos and apparent lack of order, but then he realised that Walt had left a metaphorical trail of giant breadcrumbs and all he, Jeffrey, had to do was to follow the path.

And I guess if my words of wisdom are ever going to be good for anything, it's a trail of breadcrumbs just for you, in case you are ever unsure, in case you can't remember, in case I'm not around to check with.

But, actually, even if you forget about this for ever, the bottom line is this: even when I am not with you, I am always going to be with you. There is never going to be a day that you do not make my heart beat, never going to be a day when I am not living and breathing with Love for you; never a day when I am not bursting with pride at just being your dad.

And if, just if, there is ever an unmentionable day when I am not around, well then recall these words from the wonderful A.A. Milne:

> If ever there is tomorrow when we're not together . . .
> there is something you must always remember. You
> are braver than you believe, stronger than you seem,
> and smarter than you think. But the most important
> thing is, even if we're apart . . . I'll always be with you.

And that's the truth of it. There has never been, nor will there ever be, a time when I do not Love you with my whole heart. And when I am no longer here and you have only the memory of me, my Love for you will remain, unending, unceasing, always constant. When you see rays of sunlight dancing through breaks in the clouds, you will know that I am watching you and loving you, always.

Now, while we all recover from that unseemly, and let's be honest quite vulgar, outburst of emotion and blow our noses, let us reflect for a moment on the life you are going to live.

The wonderful T.H. Mordaunt wrote,

> Sound, sound the clarion; fill the fife,
> Throughout the sensual world proclaim,
> One crowded hour of glorious life,
> Is worth an age without a name.

So there you have it, guys: live your lives as though you have nothing to fear, as though you have nothing to lose, as if nothing can go wrong. Let every day's activity be a great adventure and always be guided by Love.

Because if you do, your lives will be truly remarkable.

But above all else, and I know that you know this, always remember that I Love you; I really, really Love you,

Dad x

WARMEST THANKS

As with every project, many people helped to bring *The 50 Things* to fruition and I want to thank them all for their help and support, not least my wife Joanna who is possibly the kindest person I have ever met and who, when I announced that I was dragging my computer to a nook at the other end of the house for a year to do some writing, merely raised an eyebrow and continued with whatever she was doing at the time. Thank you, darling Jo.

I also need to thank the brilliant Dotti Irving and the magical Clare Conville for managing this whole process, which from my perspective has been as easy as falling off a log. They introduced me to an editor, the gentle but incisive Gillian Stern, who helped me to hone this book. Additionally I must thank the sparkling Anna Valentine at Trapeze who embraced *The 50 Things* with a passion, and to whom I am eternally grateful for fulfilling one of my life's ambition; I must also thank her marketing whizz Anna Bowen for coming up with the subtitle when I could not. I'm also indebted to the entire Trapeze/Orion team for giving me a home and letting this idea live beyond its original iteration.

Lastly, I must thank my friends and family who read the original blog on which this book is based and encouraged me to keep going with it: if I have forgotten you, I apologise but I need to thank my friend, the amazing Richard Ashworth whose inspirational words always gets me to the point; my surrogate parents

Charlie and Janet Baker for being totally solid when the chips were really down; my great friend Steve Bertram with whom I discussed the original idea and who inspired me to turn my mid-life crisis into something much more positive; the brilliant Edward Bulmer whose comments were so insightful and so clear; my beautiful god-daughter Hannah Dowie for reading and commenting on every single post; my father Lee Dunne and his amazing wife Maura and my wonderful sister Sarah and brother-in-law John Fenton for their ongoing support of both the project and me, generally; Saffron Guy who supported it from the outset; my old friend Hugh Jackman who pushed me to publish; darling Chrissie Rucker who shared the blog with her White Company mailing list; and Stephen Russell (aka The Barefoot Doctor) for showing me how to lean back; deliberately leaving the most important until last: my dearest and oldest friend Andrew Dowie who has had to put up with my crap since we were fourteen and is still smiling. Bless you all.